Praise for *Uncommon Beauty*

"Margaret Meder provides guidance and information to help parents cope and move forward, making the best decisions possible to care for their medically fragile children, their families, and themselves. . . . *Uncommon Beauty* touches the soul and nourishes the spirit."

—Deborah Segersten, MSN, RN Clinical Nurse Manager, Trauma and Trauma/Surgical IMC, UWHC Madison WI

"While advocating for her child and maneuvering through complex healthcare systems, Margaret Meder learned many lessons. She shares them here and provides concrete suggestions to help other parents cope with the emotional, psychosocial, and financial challenges of caring for a child with special healthcare needs, providing insights that only a parent who has walked that path could offer."

—Barbara J. Byrne, DNP, RN, PNP-BC, Director of Pediatric Nursing and Clinical Services, American Family Children's Hospital

"This wise and beautifully written book provides a practical roadmap for parents navigating the first few years of 'crisis parenting' with a medically fragile child. I recommend *Uncommon Beauty* to parents, caregivers, healthcare professionals, and anyone interested in a story of courage, strength, and amazing resilience."

—Erica Serlin, PhD, Family Therapy Center of Madison, Adjunct Clinical Faculty-Department of Psychiatry and Psychology, University of Wisconsin–Madison

UNCOMMON
beauty

CRISIS PARENTING FROM DAY ONE

MARGARET MEDER

BEAVER'S
POND
PRESS

ISBN 13: 978-1-59298-487-9

Library of Congress Catalog Number: 2012908590

Printed in the United States of America

First Printing: 2012

16 15 14 13 12   5 4 3 2 1

Cover photography by *artessence*.
Inside back cover portrait by Terry Stanley
Cover and interior design by James Monroe Design, LLC.

Beaver's Pond Press
7108 Ohms Lane
Edina, MN 55439–2129
952-829-8818
www.BeaversPondPress.com

BEAVER'S
POND
PRESS

To order, visit www.BeaversPondBooks.com
or call 1-800-901-3480. Reseller discounts available.

To all of the parents just starting their journey
with their own uncommonly beautiful children.
You are not alone.

CONTENTS

CONTENTS

CONTENTS

AUTHOR NOTE

During the early years of caring for Evan, our lives lost any sense of neat organization that we may have once achieved. Each day was unpredictable. The luxury of moving from one moment to the next in a smooth and logical fashion fell away. One moment I'd be all set to leave for work; the next moment I'd drop everything and run for the ER.

Life stops while we are stationed at the hospital. After Evan's needs are met, there are Jonathan's needs, and finally the parents' needs. Somewhere in the midst of everything, we spend time accepting our new life and planning for our future. It is a jarring, back-and-forth focus of attention.

By nature I long for organization and reason. To that end I have organized my experiences and ideas in as logical a sequence as possible, which means that my journal entries are arranged by topic, and not by date. In reality there is very little that can be predictable, organized, or smooth flowing when a member of a family has special healthcare needs.

Everything presented here is based on my personal experiences. The information in this book is not intended to be a complete directory of advice or resources for all parents in all circumstances. My intention is to share some basic information that I have learned from my experiences. Programs, laws, systems, and medical care can vary by family, by state, and over time.

INTRODUCTION

Sunday morning, June 13, 2004, was filled with the excitement of childbirth. It was time to go to the hospital. We would have our baby today. I imagined snuggling our baby boy and bringing him home. I couldn't wait to meet him and see what he looked like. Randy rushed around doing the expectant dad routine. He called the doctor, bundled Jonathan off to a neighbor's house, gathered my bags, and drove us to the hospital. These would be the last normal moments for a long time to come. We did not know that today our lives would be changing in ways never imagined.

The surreal events began unfolding as a nurse pushed me into surgery. She made small talk and said, "Do you mind having a baby on the thirteenth? Some moms don't like having a baby on the thirteenth."

I hadn't thought about it. I felt a squeeze in my heart, not wanting to mar the day. "Oh no. I'm just glad the day is here."

I was scheduled to have a C-section. This baby was breech, like our first son Jonathan, now two years old. Unlike my first pregnancy, this one had been especially difficult. I had painful, at times incapacitating, back problems and gestational diabetes. Thinking another pregnancy would be risky, Randy and I decided to have my tubes tied during the cesarean.

In surgery I felt the strong tugging of our baby being pulled out of me. I heard my doctor say, "We have a boy." But I didn't hear the baby crying. The cry is coming, I told myself. Just wait, it's coming. And the crying began. Relieved, I said, "There it is—I love that sound." I smiled and exhaled. Everything was fine, the baby was crying.

I barely heard my doctor say, "Margaret, I realize that I forgot to ask you whether, if there was a problem with the baby, you still want your tubes tied?"

I thought, *That's odd that she is asking me about some forgotten paperwork now.* I focused my thoughts and felt certain that my mind was set with the decision. "Yes." I answered.

"We'll get this little guy wrapped up and we'll bring him to meet you," she said in a way that eased my mind.

My doctor came to my side. Her face was sober as she said, "Margaret, I couldn't tie your tubes today."

Naively I thought, *Didn't you have the right tools?*

She continued, "There are some problems with the baby."

I couldn't breathe, feeling a hot panic growing inside of me.

"The baby's head is misshapen; his forehead is like a hood curving forward over his face."

What? How could my baby's head look like that? Will he live?

"His fingers and toes didn't form correctly and there are some other problems, too."

Fingers didn't form correctly? No!

I felt numb as I looked at Randy.

"Dad can hold him next to you for a minute, and then we'll need to get him quickly to the neonatal intensive care unit."

I watched Randy gingerly take our tiny son and bring him close to me. We weren't prepared to comfort our distressed baby as our own tears fell. We cradled him, trying to feel joy instead of the heaviness that was pressing down on us. We fearfully looked at his head while lovingly embracing him. Our child. He didn't look like our child. We listened to him whimper; desperately wishing we could make everything right. The nurse took him away and we were left to begin life as parents of a medically fragile child.

Our lives took on new meaning that we wouldn't fully understand for years. We learned that Evan had a rare craniofacial condition called Apert syndrome. This rare genetic syndrome causes skeletal abnormalities, including premature fusing of sutures in the skull, fused fingers and toes, wide-set and protruding eyes, and a sunken mid-face. A wide range of other conditions can be present. For Evan this also includes a curved spine, fusion of neck vertebrae, abnormal shoulder bones, respiratory issues, digestive issues, moderate hearing loss, and impaired vision.

The ultrasounds didn't show anything that alerted the doctors to a definite problem. But even if they had, we really couldn't have been prepared. The red flags that showed up were dismissed as within normal parameters: closed fists that didn't reveal individual fingers, a slightly larger head than normal, excess amniotic fluid. We were told there was nothing out of the ordinary for us to be concerned about.

To understand the challenges we faced in our new roles as parents of a medically fragile child, think of the typical new parent's level of self-doubt, frustration, exhaustion, and general lack of knowledge about parenting. Then enlarge that unknown body of information to include everything you possibly have to know about living a life that includes sole responsibility for a child with complicated health conditions that you will have to understand and treat, forever. This is the learning curve that we had in front of us. We were confronted with making decisions about life-and-death matters we knew nothing about. On top of that, most of Evan's doctors had never treated a child with Apert syndrome.

While sad and grieving, we couldn't have predicted the joy that would come from this special boy. While isolated and alone, we couldn't imagine that we would develop deeper bonds of friendship than we had ever known before. While afraid, we couldn't have dreamed of becoming pillars of strength. While in pain, we couldn't have known that we were discovering how to be compassionate. While enduring seemingly endless difficulties, we couldn't know that we were learning true patience. While questioning the reasons for our struggles, we would be astounded by wonderful and unexplainable miracles.

In the first weeks and months I longed for a guidebook. Something to hold that offered ideas and positive thoughts. I went to a bookstore for my first outing away from the hospital. I looked for answers to the challenges that I was facing. I found happy books about bringing baby home, setting up routines, creating the perfect growing and learning environment. I found sad books with long painful stories about when something went wrong. I found technical books that dealt with specific conditions different from ours. The book that I was looking for would have practical ideas about how to manage our new life, facts about working with doctors and hospitals, tips that only seasoned caregivers knew, revelations that would validate my emotions and reactions, affirmations of hope, and answers to the mysteries of caring for our child. This book would be easy to read with short essays that could be quickly taken in with the few spare moments I might have during a busy day. I couldn't find my guidebook; it didn't exist. I left empty-handed and discouraged.

As our days continued on, we gradually became knowledgeable and competent parents for Evan. We learned through experience and research. We had many people who helped to guide us. We watched miracles take place, setting in stone our faith in God and the goodness all around us.

I have been compelled for some time to create the book I longed for, collecting ideas and stories with each new experience. My goal is to make someone else's life easier by sharing what I have learned. While every medically fragile child's condition is unique, what we have learned could be applied to many situations. I hope that you will find answers, validation, ideas, and hope in these pages.

one

SURVIVING THE
FIRST DAYS

Rise to the Challenge

Still in the delivery room, we gaze at Evan. The heaviness pressing down on us threatens the first moment of joy at finally seeing our baby. Randy holds him gently and lifts one of Evan's little mitten hands for us to examine. Evan's face is scrunched up and his precious eyes are shut tight against the light that has just broken into his life. He whimpers and we murmur soft sounds back to him.

Evan is whisked off to the NICU (neonatal intensive care unit). I am moved to a recovery room; Randy and my doctor follow behind. The doctor takes Randy aside and speaks to him alone.

"You have to be really strong now. You have a big job to do, taking care of your family. You are going to have to help Margaret get through this while she recovers. It is up to you to stay with Evan and watch over his care and make sure he gets everything he needs. It's going to be hard. You are going to have to rise to the challenge."

Randy takes her advice to heart and remains vigilant. We are stunned and in shock, but he stays strong. He watches over Evan and delivers updates to me. He calls a few close relatives and friends, in between checking on Evan and me. We continue this way for several days, bewildered by what our life has become.

Take Time to Experience Your Emotions

Like every expectant parent, we had spent months dreaming about our life with our new baby. Apart from fleeting moments of worry, we had spent our time dreaming about the healthy baby we would soon be holding and nurturing. We had imagined cozy scenes of our new family in our carefully prepared home.

Now we found ourselves faced with the very profound loss of our dreams, coupled with daunting new challenges. Like us, you may find yourself aching with emotions that you aren't prepared for as your life becomes something very different from the life you dreamed of.

Two hours old

I bury myself in my bed, hiding my sobs and my tear-swollen face. I try to hold in my pain by curling into a tight ball. I can't control my emotions. Randy comes and goes between my room and the nursery. He doesn't have the luxury of being able to hide away from the world, like I can.

I am devastated over Evan's complicated physical anomalies and health challenges. I have visions of us spending the rest of our lives caring for a disabled child. I see the picture of my perfect family dissolve into a blurry strangeness. I think about all the normal kid things that Evan might not ever do. I am afraid that we will be shunned by the world. It is hard for Randy and me to actually say these things out loud to each other—the weight of both of us in agony at the same time is unbearable. We trade off being strong.

A nurse consoles me, "Take time now to grieve the loss of what you dreamed your life with your baby would be like. Just about everything you imagined is different now. If you take time now, it will help you to heal and make new dreams. It is okay to grieve the loss of all those dreams and plans." This advice allows me to direct my grief towards how I had imagined our life would be, without directing the feelings toward Evan. I cry for two days straight, until I feel a quiet numbness. At least now I can get out of my bed and leave my room.

If you allow yourself time to grieve the loss of what you had imagined, there is a future for your family, a different one than you planned for, but still full of promise for great things. Through Evan's sweet disposition and his captivating personality, I have discovered richer life experiences than I ever could have imagined before he was born.

Start a Notebook

I began writing information notebooks the day Evan was born. Every bit of information I learn goes into this one location. By doing this one simple thing, I have had a wealth of information about my child's medical history at my fingertips.

Consider starting this immediately, if you haven't done it already. Get a small spiral notebook and write down everything in this one place. Choose a small one that is easy to carry. Keep it with you at all times.

When the entire notebook is used up, start a new one. Assign a number to each book to track the timeline. Save all the old notebooks and refer back for important information. These notebooks are one of my most valuable tools.

Five hours old

Randy says the doctor is coming in to talk to us. They think they know what is wrong with Evan, something called Apert syndrome. I pick up my notebook and we brace ourselves for the news. I write the words "Apert syndrome." Nothing feels real anymore. The doctor comes in and starts talking. I take notes: "Characteristics of Apert: craniosynostosis, fused fingers and toes. Other conditions present. Trouble breathing—intubated." She shows us pictures of children with the distinctive facial features of Apert syndrome (large head, protruding and wide-set eyes, misshapen teeth). We can hardly breathe, thinking that Evan might possibly grow up to look so different.

Write notes on everything related to your child's care in the notebook.

- Names and phone numbers for nurses, doctors, important contacts

- Medical terms

- Notes on conversations with specialists

- Medicines, dosages, and times given

- Record of patterns (e.g.: always coughs while eating, times of meals, difficult nights, and what happened the previous day)

- Questions as you think of them, so you don't forget

- Insurance conversations (date, time, representative's name, everything discussed, and a reference number for the call)

- Inspirational moments that you want to remember

- Date of every hospital admittance

- Summary of significant health events

Do Some Research

We quickly realized that we had a lot of work ahead of us in understanding Evan's condition and figuring out treatment plans for a multitude of health problems. Soon the doctors began giving their recommendations and we had decisions to make.

Prepare yourself to make the decisions ahead by doing your research, understanding the conditions and accompanying issues, and knowing all the possible solutions.

One day old, early morning

Randy forges ahead with gathering information about Apert syndrome and all of the accompanying issues. He needs to keep busy while I am recovering and Evan is in the NICU. He searches the web, reads books, talks with nurses and doctors. He begins to develop an understanding of what we will need to do to care for all of Evan's complicated health issues.

Randy finds the website Apert.org which is a hub of activity for families with Apert syndrome. At this website we find resources and we connect with other parents. These experienced parents answer many of our questions. They have already been through everything we are now going through, too.

A nurse tells Randy about a local family she remembers who also had a baby with Apert syndrome. She locates the family and contacts them for us. We are able to meet the family during one of their visits to the craniofacial center. They allow us to shadow them on their son's craniofacial team checkups. The concept of a team approach to treat a medical condition is completely new to us and shadowing them on their appointments helps us understand how Evan's condition will be treated.

Don't get discouraged or frustrated if you ask questions and the answer is, "I don't know." The answers are out there; keep searching. When we asked our first attending physician if it would be possible to have Evan's fingers separated, the answer was, "I don't know." We were discouraged, but kept on searching. When we asked the first specialist we found, the answer was, "We can reconstruct some of his fingers, and it will take many surgeries." That wasn't good enough—Evan needed all of his fingers. We kept searching. When we asked the second specialist we found, the one we flew 1,000 miles to see, the answer was, "Yes, we can separate all of his fingers in two surgeries." That was the answer we were looking for.

Don't expect to find all the answers and specialists in your own town. You might have to travel, even if you live in a large metropolitan area. Because Evan's syndrome is rare and there are few specialists in the entire country who have experience treating this condition, we have had to travel a lot. We regularly visit specialty healthcare facilities in other cities and even other states.

Doing this type of work for a special needs child is like being a detective. You do research, uncover clues, find leads, investigate, discover possible solutions, and make informed decisions.

Work Put on Hold

Of course, everybody's work situation is different. Fortunately we had careers with flexibility and understanding coworkers. We had planned for our maternity leave before we knew everything that would transpire with Evan's birth. Mine was simple to arrange. I was giving private music lessons, and my students were prepared to take an eight-week hiatus from lessons whenever our baby was born. Randy would be teaching summer school. We relied on this income to get us through the summer, so he planned to take only a few days off when the baby was born. I planned to do my best to make a quick recovery from a caesarian section in order to carry on at home with Randy at work during the days.

However, Evan came three weeks earlier than expected and was overflowing with complications. We definitely needed more than a few days from Randy. His colleagues genuinely wanted to contribute to our cause. They created a plan to substitute teach his class for several weeks, allowing Randy to still earn the paycheck we desperately needed, especially now.

I sent an email to my students, saying I was putting lessons on hold until sometime in the fall. I hoped to be able to start teaching in mid-September (twelve weeks away). However, I couldn't guarantee that I would be able to teach again. All of my students stayed on with me, waiting patiently for the time when I might be able to work again.

If you find that you need to take time off to care for your child, do some research. Check into the *Family and Medical Leave Act*, and check the US Department of Labor website for more details: www.dol.gov/whd/fmla/. Find out if your employer has a "bank" in which employees can donate their unused vacation or sick days. If you have short-term disability insurance, find out if your policy offers paid leave to care for an ill family member.

Safety Nets

As you become aware of the grief and the pressures you face, you will have to develop coping strategies. Chapter 6, Caring for Yourself, explores a wide range of personal care strategies (such as pacing yourself, positive affirmations, prayer, meditation, and exercise). However, it may take time to get to a point where you are able to focus on yourself and develop these strategies.

One coping strategy you might be thinking about now is taking an antidepressant/antianxiety medication. Consider that we are in a time when the prevalence of postpartum depression with "normal" births is widely recognized. Imagine how the birth of a medically fragile child has an even greater potential to bring about or intensify postpartum depression. As one part of a whole regime of survival techniques, medication might give you some immediate relief to move ahead with your life.

Starting any medication is a personal choice, with many considerations to be thought through. Some people are philosophically opposed to these types of medications. Others believe that psychiatric drugs have their place in treating people who are suffering from stress and other mental health issues. And there are some that may have other underlying health conditions that contraindicate their ability to take these medications. Only you and your doctor can decide whether or not this choice might be right for you.

I bring up the topic of antidepressant/antianxiety medications because, like everything else in this book, it is part of my experience. This crisis promised to tax every fiber in my body. As I plummeted into grief, I chose to try medication. I needed a safety net, something to catch me and pull me back up. I needed to be able to function in this precarious new situation. I proceeded knowing that if I didn't like the effect of the medication I could stop it at any time. I had a lot to gain, with very little to lose.

One day old, midmorning

Amidst my grief, my doctor visits me to see how I am doing. She looks almost as exhausted as I feel. I realize that this day has been hard on her, too. I explain that I am not sure how I will cope. She asks me if I want to consider taking an antidepressant and/or a sedative to help me sleep. I hesitate and ask what impact the medications will have on breast milk. She assures me that it is safe; it won't have any effect on that. I decide to start the medications, hoping that they will help me get in control of my emotions so that I can do what needs to be done and get some rest.

I start out with two medications. I suspect that the "sedative" medication is making me feel dizzy and out of it, as if I am walking in a dream. So I stop that medication after a few days and come out of the haze I have been in. But I keep taking the antidepressant and I gradually begin to notice that I feel stronger. I notice that I am not as anxious in situations where I normally would be. I am not crying as much and I am not falling to pieces with every piece of alarming news. I am feeling joy in my new baby, challenges and all. I am able to face surgeries, procedures, and daily crises. While the relief I experience from the medication doesn't make everything right, it does help me begin to function and do what needs to be done.

If you think an antidepressant or antianxiety medication might help you through this period, talk to your doctor. You will not be the first new mother to have this conversation. You are simply considering all the possibilities that will make your life doable for you, and you are developing your plan of many strategies that will carry you through your new life.

Evan's Pediatrician

One day old, afternoon

A nurse steps into my room and informs me that our pediatrician is here. She wants to visit me, if I am feeling up to it. I am surprised, but also impressed that she would visit me now. The hospital doctors had been supervising Evan's care, and I wasn't expecting her. She enters my room and sits in the chair next to my bed. Full of compassion, she asks about Evan and me. I share the little information I know. She says she is available for us whenever we need her. For now, the hospital will be caring for Evan, but I can contact her whenever I need to. She comforts me and assures me that she will be there for me.

Wires and Tubes

There are few things as sobering as seeing your child covered with wires and tubes. He looks so delicate, so vulnerable. The wires, tubes, tapes, and incubators are an intimidating weave of artificial umbilical cords—more science fiction than reality—creating barriers that separate us from our baby. Every strand has a function; understanding this brings peace.

One day old, afternoon

It is my shift now. Randy has left to try to get some sleep and he will spend time with Jonathan, our two-year-old son, who is at home protected from all of this.

I sit next to Evan, scared to even stroke his cheek for fear that I might disrupt something. I relax into a daze, waiting. An alarm goes off, jolting me into a panic. A nurse comes in and adjusts this or that and resets the machines. She leaves. I stay and return to a daze. The cycle of waiting, falling into a daze, jolting awake, resetting of machines continues.

Some of my uneasiness dies away as I realize that all the tapes and bandages are not actually covering wounds or treating any injury. They are just holding the wires and tubes in place. And the wires aren't actually going into Evan's body. The wires are just resting on his skin to monitor his heart rate, breathing, oxygen saturation levels. For the most part they have been delivering good news.

I become comfortable with the IV. This is just a needle connected to a tube delivering fluids and medicines. That's good—he needs that.

I can accept the NG tube [nasogastric feeding tube] in his nose, too. He is getting food and that is all that matters.

The intubation tube, the big wide tube going into his mouth is the hardest to accept. It looks so invasive—so bulky—life support at its most basic. Moving air in and out of his lungs because he can't breathe on his own.

I take a big breath, reach in and touch his cheek. My baby is alive.

One week after he is born, the intubation tube comes out. All of the remaining tubes and wires are gathered into a big awkward bundle, he is lifted gingerly out of the incubator and first into my lap and then into Randy's. Finally, parents and baby united. Our eyes connect and we begin to bond.

Eventually, as the days go by, we will become mostly immune to the wires and tubes, although they still taunt us with their life-sustaining power. We can nimbly gather the bundle in our hands, carefully avoiding pulling anything out of its place—or worse, stepping on anything—and scoop Evan into our arms ourselves. No alarms go off. We are a team, Evan fighting, parents cheering him on all the way.

Permission to Step Back

Give yourself permission to step back from the bombardment of information. Gathering information and understanding what you are dealing with is your main task right now. But take breaks when you need to—all the information can wait, for a little while.

Two days old

I feel exhausted. Physically exhausted from giving birth. Mentally exhausted from learning all this new information. Emotionally exhausted from receiving this unexpected, huge, gigantic, life-altering change of plans. I know that Evan is seriously impaired. But actually lumping him into the category of "children having Apert syndrome" feels like I am giving in to the reality of this situation too quickly. I can almost believe his diagnosis, but not quite. I am not ready to condemn Evan to what seems like such a bleak future.

Randy diligently searches out information and shares it with me, trying desperately to understand what we are dealing with. I tell him that I can't look at it now. He understands, and I feel like a terrible parent. The barrage of information makes me feel like I am being forced to give my mandatory acceptance, now. But I'm not ready—I need more time. I hate myself for saying "Just put it down; I can't look at it right now," or "Okay" when someone tells me something but I don't really hear it. As my emotions calm, I begin to face the truth—the reality of what we are dealing with. Bit by bit we study the articles and information. Just a little at a time. The moments of acceptance grow longer and less painful, until we fully own the title of "parents of a child with Apert syndrome."

When you feel like you are overflowing with information and you can't process another thing, put it all aside. Put aside the scientific articles, books, and doctor's notes. Rest your mind. Give yourself time to move through the grieving process. In my experience, denial comes first and acceptance comes last. You will learn everything you need to know, in time.

One Hour at a Time

When you are overwhelmed, concentrate on the present moment and the one thing that most needs your absolute immediate attention.

There is a lot of work ahead of you and you can't do everything at once. Choose whatever is most important and start doing it. No matter how much you finish, there will always be more to do. Say to yourself, "Take it one hour at a time" or even "one minute at a time." Really mean it when you say it, and do whatever you can with the minute or hour that you have. Then put your other concerns off to the side. They will be there, ready to be taken up again when you have the time.

I learn to keep myself grounded by reminding myself to think about the true reality of the moment. I keep myself from creating "what if" scenarios that are only figments of my imagination. It is all too easy to put so much pressure on myself worrying that I render myself useless.

To create a calmer mindset and relieve anxiety I say to myself, "I can make it through this, one minute at a time."

To stop a panic attack, when there isn't any immediate threat to life, I say to myself, "This isn't an emergency; right now at this moment we are all fine."

To get started on a difficult task I say to myself, "I can do anything for a few minutes."

To remind myself that it doesn't all have to get done in one fell swoop I say to myself, "It won't be the end of the world if this doesn't get done today."

To accept the reality of time constraints, I say to myself, "This is one thing that isn't going to get done."

All you have to do is get through this one minute, one thing at a time. Eventually you will get through every day, accomplishing the most important things, one by one.

Time Can Heal

Sometimes the best action is to wait and watch. Sometimes the human body can heal itself.

Two days old

Evan has developed fluid around his heart. His condition is now too complicated to be treated in the hospital where he was born. He needs to be at the University Hospital, where there are more of the resources needed for his care. The doctor says they hope to move him as soon as possible, with our permission. I am seized with panic. After taking in how serious that sounds—fluid around his heart—I realize that the University Hospital is an hour away and I'll still be here, recovering from the C-section. I can't bear the thought of him being taken so far away from my reach. What if he needs me? What if something terrible happens to him and I can't be there?

Of course we have no choice. He has to go and I have to stay. Randy goes with him to the new hospital. We are separated for a day. But the thought of getting to Evan is the best motivation I can have to force my quick recovery. I push myself to get up and get moving.

Once Evan is settled into the University Hospital NICU, we are informed of a new health problem nearly every day. He continues to be intubated, has developed jaundice, isn't digesting his food, and still has the fluid around his heart. The doctors evaluate his heart condition and decide that the best course of action is to watch him, monitor the fluid, and wait until it is absolutely necessary to intervene. It would be an invasive procedure to remove the fluid and the doctors aren't ready to take the risk.

After several days of watching and monitoring, the doctors deliver good news that sounds like a miracle to us: the fluid around Evan's heart has disappeared; it has been absorbed by his body. His heart is working well now, without the extra stress of the fluid buildup.

Always leave room in your heart and mind for the possibility of a miracle.

FAMILY AND FRIENDS

Overflowing with Love and Support

Five days old

We find ourselves overflowing with love and support. In our most difficult time, our family and friends are lifting us up, easing our burden in every way imaginable.

Our family calls often—short calls just to hear our voices. They are shocked and devastated by the news. They have been blessed with healthy babies for as long as they can remember. Parents, sisters, brothers, even cousins, make plans to travel across the country to visit us, hoping they can help in some way. Evan is embraced—our family determined to celebrate his birth and do whatever they can to support us.

Neighbors and friends take Jonathan on play dates and keep him overnight. They bring him fun things to play with and keep up his spirits. They bring us food and inspirational gifts.

Our church friends immediately go into action, organizing babysitters, mowing our lawn, making quilts, and planning meals.

Colleagues bring presents, give us their encouragement, and wait quietly to hear news.

Unbelievably, there are more than fifty names on a list of people to thank, in just the first three weeks. We are being sustained through our darkest days. Our hearts are comforted and we can keep going without totally giving in to despair. We are thankful for a world that is full of good people and love.

Streamline Communications

Communicating with friends and family during a crisis brings tremendous comfort. It's a top priority. But don't be surprised if you find that staying in touch with all of your supporters often takes more time and energy than you have. Streamlining your communications is really important.

A few websites have been developed to provide communication solutions for individuals faced with serious illnesses. They provide a place where everyone can go to find the latest updates.

Two outstanding websites are www.carepages.com and www.caringbridge.org. On these websites you will be able to set up your own page where you can post updates and pictures. Friends and family who join your page receive email notices when you post an update. In return they can send messages of support.

These websites provide a private place solely for the purpose of supporting the patient and family. No outside chatter about other events or issues enter into the dialogue. These sites have a different tone than social networks such as Facebook. You will also find resources for surviving a health crisis and information on various healthcare issues.

Our website updates have also become a journal of events for us, keeping track of the challenges and milestones along the way. Randy is the journal writer for our CarePages updates. Our spirits are lifted reading the messages from our family and friends during our most trying times.

Seven days old

CarePages Posted June 20, 2004, 8:25 p.m.

Today was pretty good. Evan was taken off the ventilator, although they have to watch him closely to see how he handles breathing on his own. His airway is probably a little swollen from having a tube in it for a whole week, causing him to have to work harder to breathe right now. They may still need to give him a little oxygen to help things along, but hopefully they will not have to intubate him again.

Jonathan had a good time again with his baby-sitter this afternoon. He has been such a good boy, and we are so proud of the way he has behaved for all of the people who have been taking care of him.

For those of you who do not already know, many friends and neighbors have been taking care of Jonathan (our two-year-old) while we spend time with Evan.

We are so thankful for all the help from our friends here, and for all of the thoughts and prayers (and emails) from our friends and family far away from us. You are all helping us so much through this very difficult time.

Dearest Randy and Margaret, We are all watching in wonder at you and your two gems. We are admiring your pearls as they reveal themselves in Evan and Jonathan, through the love and devotion of his awe-inspiring parents. Love, Mother

Nine days old

CarePages Posted June 22, 2004, 8:30 a.m.

Evan has been off the intubation ventilator for almost two days and he seems to be handling it pretty well. Mommy and Daddy both held him on Monday, which was a great joy. There are a few new photos of us holding him in the gallery. We can't wait until we can hold him whenever we want to.

He had an upper G.I. test Monday to see why he wasn't digesting food, and the problem may have been his feeding tube blocking the entrance to his intestines. The doctors pulled the tube back a bit and will try giving him some milk soon to see if it gets beyond his stomach.

We still do not know when he will be able to come home with us, but we hope to know more within the next few days.

You're always in our thoughts, Randy, Margaret, Jonathan, and Evan. We think about you all the time and are praying for Evan to continue being a strong little trooper. We can't wait to meet him! Thanks for continuing to keep us updated on Evan's daily progress. Hugs to all of you! Love, Mike & Lisa

What Do I Say?

What do you say to someone who is faced with this type of crisis? Friends and family will struggle with what to say and do. They want to provide comfort and support. The ideas below may provide a window into your world for onlookers searching for the right words.

What we have needed most is to know that we are not alone in this experience. Nobody can change the painful truth of our experience, but you can be there for us by saying, "I am here for you."

"I love you and I will be here when you need me."

"I will support you, let me help."

"What do you need?"

Keep in touch and remind us that you are holding us in your heart. We need to know that we are not being abandoned.

Tread carefully when you feel compelled to say anything that intellectualizes the situation or speculates about the possible meaning of this tragedy. Words like, "This is a divine plan and there is a reason why," imply that God intentionally inflicted these struggles on a defenseless baby in order to teach a lesson. Right now, I can't comprehend that my child's pain and deformities could possibly be someone else's divine plan. In time, these words may bring comfort to some people, but not yet, not in the beginning. Maybe later, when we can see the bigger picture in action.

Ten days old

I am home from the hospital to take a shower and to change into fresh clothes. The house is quiet. I feel empty and alone. Sighing, I walk into the nursery and finger the sweet blankets and soft clothes. It's not fair.

I go into to my office to try to be productive and organize a few papers. Not really wanting to hear the phone messages, I play them anyway. A call from my sister, saying she is thinking about us. A call from the church, saying they are organizing meals. A call from an acquaintance saying, "I just want you to know that I'm thinking about you. I can't think of any other parents better than you guys to have a special-needs baby. You guys are the perfect people for this. (Is she implying that while this would have been way too much for other parents, it is just right for us?) Good luck. I'm thinking of you." I know she meant well, but it wasn't what I needed to hear at that time. And that was pretty much it. I didn't hear from her again. She was busy doing normal things with her normal family, and I was busy doing the not-normal things with my not-normal family, devastated by a tragedy that was apparently "just right for us."

Help us through our experience with frequent reminders that we are not alone; do not abandon us. We are discovering that humanity and being connected to others are the things that make this new life a triumph instead of a tragedy.

Accept Help from Family and Friends

Imagine how you felt when you were able to help someone else in need. Maybe you delivered a meal to a sick friend, gave a thoughtful gift, provided some childcare, ran an errand. Being able to give to someone in need can be one of life's most rewarding experiences.

On the other hand, needing and accepting help from others can be one of life's most humbling experiences. Most people would agree it is easier to give than to receive. You may feel very uncomfortable accepting help from friends and family. But consider this; sometimes the greatest gift you can give a friend is to allow that friend to help you. That is how powerful the experience of giving truly is.

It is easiest to accept an offer to help when it is something specific, such as, "I would like to bring you supper tonight." Less specific offers, "How can I help?" are more challenging.

Start by making a list of all the things that someone else could do for you.

- Laundry
- Meals
- Babysitting
- Lawn mowing
- Shopping
- Errands

If someone offers to help, say "Thank you. I really appreciate that. I have a list of things that I haven't been able to do, could I show it to you?" Share the list with them and let them choose how they might help you.

Acts of Kindness

Amidst the challenges and hardships that you face, you may receive acts of kindness that you never expected. Friends and family will give you support and want to know what you need. Friends of friends who heard your story, people you don't even know, might show up wanting to help. You can accept these acts of kindness, knowing that they are gifts from the heart.

Eleven days old

I turn my attention to the gift bag in front of me. Evan is sleeping and I have a quiet moment to myself. My friend Maria is watching Jonathan today. He will play with her kids and they will have a happy time together. She sent a little gift bag for me to have in the hospital, filled with little surprises: a book filled with quotations of hope, energy bars, a sandwich, a bottle of tea. I feel her presence with me even though I am sequestered in Evan's hospital room. I imagine the carefree times we spent together not too long ago, before all of this happened to me. It is comforting eating the lunch she has sent along and reading the little book of hope. This book fortifies my resolve to keep going and becomes one of my most cherished distractions in uncertain times.

How friends and family can help

- Provide meals and baskets of fruit.
- Give care packages with energy bars and light reading.
- Pick up lunch to share at the hospital.
- Show up with a surprise cup of coffee.
- Send gas cards or other gift cards.
- Babysit older children.
- Arrange play dates for older children.
- Give care packages for older children.
- Help with laundry and housekeeping.
- Plant a small therapy garden.
- Give a hair salon or spa gift certificate.
- Mow the lawn.
- Stop by for short visits to "keep watch" so you can sleep.
- Do birthday or holiday shopping for other children.
- Run an errand.
- Provide rides to other children's activities.
- Help organize insurance papers.
- Provide pro bono legal services with health insurance issues.
- Print off thank-you cards for quick and easy acknowledgments.
- Travel to appointments with you.
- Share frequent flyer miles if traveling by air to appointments.
- Donate vacation or sick days (coworkers).

Designate a Care Coordinator

Consider designating one person to coordinate offers to help. There may be someone in your life who would be happy to offer this kind of help. When you are in a crisis, coordinating and utilizing offers to help can feel like more work than it's worth. Don't let this prevent you from accepting help that might be available.

Twelve days old

Libby, a friend from our church, meets with us. She has offered to coordinate meals and volunteers who want to help us. She has made several months' worth of calendars. We talk about what our needs are and make a list of things we could use help with. Anyone who calls or emails offering to help is directed to Libby. She keeps the calendars filled. We are relieved and grateful.

Through this scheduling we are able to spend close to three months caring for Evan in the hospital and still have our two-year-old son's needs met. Libby arranges volunteers to babysit Jonathan during the day so that we can continue working and staying with Evan in the hospital. We are provided with meals, laundry help, yard work help, and gift cards. All this generosity saves us. It helps bridge the gaps that this unexpected crisis has created—financially, logistically, and spiritually.

Think about someone close to you that would be good at organizing help for you. If you are uncomfortable asking someone to do this for you, present the idea as something you read about in a book that sounds like it would be really helpful to you in your situation. Ask if that person could be your coordinator, or if he or she would be willing to find someone to take on this role. If you belong to a church, ask if there are any groups within the church or individuals who could help you in this way.

Thank You Cards

Everybody who is helping you knows that getting you through the crisis is all that matters. Nobody is expecting a thank you card. Writing thank you cards is probably very low on your priority list, maybe not even making the list at all. But if you don't express some sort of thank you, there is the potential that it will cause self-inflicted angst that weighs heavily on you. Conversely, the act of writing a thank you card (or an email) may help create in you a positive feeling of gratitude.

Eliminate some of the burden by creating a simple preprinted note card that you can add a short sentence to and just sign. Ask a friend to do this job for you. You could consider using a postcard format, which would save money on postage.

In its simplest form, a short note could say: "Thank you for your thoughtful gesture of support. We deeply appreciate the help we are receiving from friends like you. Sincerely, the Smith Family."

Print out the cards and keep a supply with you wherever you go. Write notes during long waits in the hospital and during long waits at appointments. Sign it and, if you feel like it, write one short sentence: "The meal was delicious." If you can't keep up with this, keep an ongoing thank you list to give to a friend to help you complete.

three

HOSPITALS AND DOCTORS

What a Hospital Feels Like

One week old

I'll never completely overcome the trepidation I feel in hospitals. I feel self-conscious around the doctors and nurses—nervous that I might say or do the wrong thing. Subdued by the sterile smells, fluorescent lighting, and cold impersonal hallways and rooms—the institutional atmosphere that begs for some soft touches (aromatherapy, trickling water features, or interesting lamps).

I catch glimpses of other sick patients and their weary families. It's humbling. Without any warning, we have become one of them—members in a society that have been mostly hidden away from us—a whole community of people who are battling illness and struggling for survival. We are no longer one of the oblivious multitude out in the world, going about our normal daily life, enjoying the freedom of good health, and spared from the inconvenience of disease.

While part of me has the odd sensation that I am only a distant observer, the other part knows I am a member now and have no choice but to jump right in and function. I settle in and become part of this community. Along the way I have short conversations with others and I absorb information. I begin to learn some of the things that the more experienced members already know.

Exposed

Almost immediately, you may become aware of the diseases around you—including infectious diseases. As you realize that hospitals hold dangerous germs, the goal of going home becomes more urgent. Be absolutely diligent about washing your hands and using antibacterial lotion every time you enter or leave your child's room.

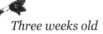

Three weeks old

The medical student intern who is assigned to Evan has been noticeably absent for days. She has spent time with us nearly every day for weeks. When she finally returns, it is obvious that she has been very sick. She says, "I got the flu that has been going around the hospital. I'm sure I caught it when I touched the elevator button with my fingertip instead of the back of my knuckle. I was in a hurry and I knew when I did it that I would end up getting sick, and I did." I tell her that I had never thought of that trick. She nods and continues, "Try not to touch your fingertips on any surfaces. Keep your fingertips as clean as possible because they end up touching your face or your food, and if there are germs on them you'll get sick. It is the same idea with using paper towels on the handle of the bathroom door when you leave. After you wash your hands, keep the paper towel and open the door handle with it, then throw away the paper towel."

If you weren't obsessive about germs before, you will be now.

Becoming Your Child's Caregiver

Too much stimulation, including a parent's touch and attention, is hard on a struggling newborn. The calm, quiet, protective environment of the NICU keeps the babies still, so they can focus all their energy on healing and growing. An unexpected touch can make them cry and flail about, send their little heart racing, and make their breathing even more difficult. Until your baby is stable, be prepared to sit by the side and be mostly hands off. Think of it as bonding delayed—not bonding denied. Your time will come.

Two weeks old

Evan is growing stronger and it is time to give him his first sponge bath. The NICU nurse suggests that I help her with this. An uneasiness has been growing inside of me—a feeling of inadequacy—will I ever be careful enough with this delicate baby? I tentatively join in, washing him gently with a sudsy washcloth and fresh water. I smile and talk to him. He is not very happy to be disturbed and lets us know with squawks and arched body, but I love every minute. I know that I will always remember this first tender moment of bathing him.

Later, I watch another mom across the room, preparing to take her baby home from the NICU. She is terrified. I don't remember seeing her in the NICU before. She must have had circumstances that prevented her from spending time at the hospital (work obligations or other children to care for). She doesn't feel prepared to take her baby home and anxiously talks with the nurse. At that moment, I couldn't have imagined taking Evan home either. I feel her fear in the core of my being as she picks up her baby and walks out the NICU doors.

In gradual steps, we learned and practiced everything we needed to know in order to be Evan's primary caregivers.

Ultimately, you will be faced with providing everything your child needs. Take this time now, while you still have the nurses to instruct you and the safety net of close supervision. When the nurse says the time is right, assist with whatever task is offered to you.

NICU, PICU, or Floor

It is comforting to know that while your child is in the NICU or PICU (Pediatric Intensive Care Unit) he will have a nurse by his side at all times. You can't get any more secure than that. However, remember that this type of intensive, specialized care can only last so long. One of the main goals is to get the patient healthy enough and strong enough to either move into a room on the pediatric floor or go home. Be ready to give up the security of the NICU or PICU at some point.

As Evan grew and his needs changed, his "home" in the hospital changed. Every time Evan moved to a different hospital unit, it felt like our world was being turned upside down. Just as we would settle into a routine, learn the rules, and watch Evan make a little progress, he would be moved somewhere else: the NICU, the PICU, the floor, back to the PICU, back to the floor, home.

Two weeks old

After two weeks in the NICU, the attending physician has just told us that they are moving Evan out, first to the PICU, then to the pediatric floor. I am nervous to move him from the safety of the NICU. How can he leave this safe secure environment? Is he really ready? Will he get the care he needs?

The NICU is full. Everyday there are newborns that need to be admitted here. Evan is getting stronger and he needs less constant care; it is time for him to move and make room for other babies who are needier than he is now.

Evan moves to the PICU. It is brighter and more private than the NICU. He stays here while he continues to have bilirubin lights for his jaundice. He does well and, within a few days, he is assigned to a room on the pediatric floor.

Apprehensively, we make the move to the floor. While the constant bedside nursing is gone, the nurses come into his room frequently. Vital sign monitors with alarms (that seem to go off constantly) continue to be placed on Evan to signal the nurses immediately if there is a problem. Evan's room is right across from the nurses' station, and that is reassuring, too.

Selfishly, I discover that there are a lot of advantages for us, the parents, now that Evan is on the pediatric floor. We have more privacy and space (making it a little easier for me to pump breast milk). We can eat in the room and we can take turns spending the night in the room. It is easier for visitors to see us.

It is a new stage of caregiving for us and we take over things like diaper changes, feeding, bathing. I watch the nurses, ask lots of questions, and master techniques I will need to continue at home.

A time comes when Evan struggles with his breathing and he needs to be moved back into the PICU. Once again he receives the almost constant bedside nursing of an intensive care unit. After several days his breathing improves and he moves back to the floor.

In retrospect, I wish I could have had a more fluid attitude about where Evan would be placed in the hospital. I feared the unknown: new nurses, new routines, new doctors. I have learned how to be more flexible, to let go of my resistance to new ideas, and to just follow each path with an alert awareness.

Medications

During the first weeks when Evan seemed to develop new health problems daily, his medications were often revised. New medicines were prescribed and others were removed. I was concerned that between the changing doctors and nurses (and the rapidly increasing volume of his charts) some instructions might get lost in the shuffle.

I began to keep an ongoing list of medications that were prescribed and administered to Evan. I wrote down notes from doctors, asking them to spell the medications they were prescribing, and the dosage. When medications were brought to Evan, I asked what was being given and I wrote down dates, times, names, and dosages. By keeping my own record, I have prevented mistakes in the hospital. In any hospital, mistakes happen. Because of this truth, I recommend that you also keep an ongoing record of medications prescribed and administered to your child. If you feel an error is being made, be prepared to ask for confirmation of the accuracy of the medication.

Likewise, whenever your newborn receives immunizations (such as while in the hospital), request a record of what he received for your records. At his pediatrician's office, Evan nearly received a repeat inoculation of an immunization he had already received at the hospital. Either it didn't transfer in the records or it was recorded incorrectly. I prevented the mistake because I asked specifically what he was receiving and realized that it sounded familiar. I looked back in my notebook and found an entry with the date it was given in the hospital. The nurse was able to track down the paper trail and confirm that he had already received this dose in the hospital. We were thankful that I had my notes and a mistake was prevented.

You are the central information center for every bit of healthcare your child receives. Although your child's medical history is recorded in his chart, realize that your child's chart will be enormous. You are the sole observer of everything that your child goes through. Therefore, be proactive in gathering and sharing information.

Know the Healthcare Providers

Take the time to understand what each healthcare provider is contributing to your child's overall treatment. Until now, your knowledge of doctors may have been limited to a general practitioner, OB-GYN, or pediatrician. Now you will be working with all kinds of specialists as you tackle many health issues.

Each time you meet a new doctor or other healthcare provider, ask for a business card. If the clinician doesn't have a card, write down the clinician's information in your notebook. Ask about the healthcare professional's area of specialty. If you don't understand what the area of specialty is (for example, a pulmonologist focuses on how the lungs work), ask for more information. Write down the date that you saw the person and specific notes about what you discussed. Find out how to reach the clinician if more questions occur to you later.

It can be very confusing as many people come and go, focusing on many different issues. Keep a good record of everyone who works with your child. Consider each specialist that you meet as a potential resource in your research.

Doctors

In the hospital, a pediatrician usually supervises your child's care. This could be either the attending physician for the hospital unit or possibly your own pediatrician, depending on each hospital's policy. Typically the doctor will see each patient once a day, and be available for follow-up as needed. Find out when your child's doctor does rounds and try to be there at that time.

If your child is in a university hospital, an individual resident or team of residents (doctors completing their specialty education) may also visit and then report to the attending physicians. Additionally, other ranks of medical students with varying duties may also visit your child. During Evan's first ten weeks we had a student intern who spent time with us. Her main assignment was to interact with us in order to gain an understanding of families in a health crisis. In turn, she listened and helped us understand lots of things that the residents and attending physicians typically don't address or may not have time to discuss.

Listen carefully to everything the doctor tells you. Take notes and ask the doctor to write down unfamiliar terms, and draw diagrams as necessary. That way you can show any other health specialist working with your child exactly what this doctor said. Allow the doctor to give you his or her complete flow of thoughts before interjecting or interrupting. Then bring up any concerns or unanswered questions.

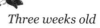

Three weeks old

Doctors don't expect you to have expertise in medicine, they just expect you to be a good parent and do your best. Don't worry about using the correct lingo; just use the words you know. I'll never know how or why the words "Do you concur?" ever came out my mouth during a discussion with two surgeons. It was the first time in my entire life that I ever said that word "concur" (definition: to express agreement). It was the first group of surgeons that I had ever spoken with, I was extremely nervous and the words just spilled out of my mouth like I said them every day, "Do you concur?" I thought, What did I just say? Did I use concur correctly? Am I going crazy? I felt an anxiety attack bubbling up as soon as I said it. But the doctors kept talking, without batting an eye. Even Randy didn't say anything—not even a surprised look. The moment passed, the meeting ended, and life went on.

It is easy to feel intimidated and anxious in a situation where you are discussing your child's complex medical conditions with a doctor. It can feel as if you, the parent, are in the spotlight, performing, and being scrutinized. It's nerve-racking and uncomfortable. If you happen to say or do something that feels ridiculous, don't beat yourself up. Be kind to yourself and understand that all people who are under stress do things that may seem slightly out of character. It's human nature. Just do your best and be able to laugh at yourself. You can take the situation seriously without taking yourself too seriously.

Second Opinions

Why is it important to get a second opinion? Because the average person's knowledge of the healthcare system is narrow and the decisions you are making are important and long lasting. How will you know what options are available if you don't do your research? You have to hear and see more than one option to make wise decisions.

It is tempting to rely on the first doctor or health center you encounter or seek out. You've invested time (a valuable commodity) into this option. You may feel as though it would be more convenient to settle for good enough. By this time you are tired and you truly want to trust what you are told. It may seem simpler to look no further because you don't want to "rock the boat." But this is your child's life, so you must push yourself to investigate all of the possibilities that are available for your child.

There are many factors to consider as you do your research.

Personality—do you respect and trust the people that you are working with? One doctor may have a personality that you like and trust (someone with compassion). Another may have a personality that makes you want to run the other way.

Expertise—is this doctor an expert in this field? How much experience does the doctor have with this particular condition? What are the doctor's credentials?

Procedures—Do you agree with the prescribed treatment? Is the treatment too aggressive or not aggressive enough?

Results—Do you know what kind of results this doctor gets? Do you have parent referrals?

Business practice—Is the practice efficient, do they respond to inquiries, do they return calls in a timely manner?

Facility—Does the facility have the best equipment available today?

Four months old

I stare at the phone in front of me. I am about to call a doctor across the country for a second opinion, and I feel like a traitor. Am I crazy to doubt the doctors who are scheduled to do surgery on Evan in just one month? They are experienced and respected in their field. They have taken Evan into their care so earnestly. It is convenient to have these doctors, right here, just an hour away.

But something doesn't feel right, and I'm just not comfortable. For one thing, one of the doctors on the team resigned from her position with the hospital in the last week. A new doctor has been assigned to the team, but he isn't a pediatric specialist. They assure me it is not a concern, but I am concerned. Another thing, I don't feel like I am connecting on any level with the surgeons; it is almost as if I am not part of the scene. My questions are not directly answered; I feel as if I am being dismissed and left to blindly follow their treatment plan. However, I'm not satisfied with the treatment plan and I need to know that I am doing the right thing for Evan. Even if all I do is validate the decision to go with this center and this surgical team, I need to get a second opinion. I need to make this call.

I pick up the phone and dial. I am so nervous. Am I going completely overboard to seek a second opinion that would mean traveling across the country to Dallas, Texas? My call is answered and I am put through to the nurse. I explain why I am calling. Her sincere interest in and knowledge of children with Apert syndrome puts me at ease. The doctor speaks with me. I am excited to hear about their treatment plans that have been successfully administered to many other patients with Apert syndrome (many patients, not just a few). I am inspired by their philosophy of treatment and dedication to improving the patient's quality of life. I make an appointment to see them two weeks from now. I hang up the phone and start making the travel arrangements.

Once we visit the Craniofacial Center in Dallas, Texas, we know that we have made the right decision. Everything feels right. Our philosophy aligns with the doctors'. The facility is magnificent. We are comforted by the presence of many other craniofacial patients—the hospital is bustling with activity. The results that we can see in other patients who are further along in the treatments are astounding. Most importantly, Evan will endure only a fraction of the surgeries that were originally prescribed. This alone is well worth the inconvenience of air travel.

Back at home, I call the local center and tell them I have decided to take Evan somewhere else. I am canceling the surgery and removing Evan from their care. They respond with a stiff admonition to rethink my decision (they aren't letting him go easily). They try to persuade us to stay—insisting that we are relying on information that is purely anecdotal, not reality. They warn us that Evan won't be able to get surgical follow-up locally. There will be too many liability issues.

But having traveled to the other center, I know the differences because I have seen them. My mind is made up. My local pediatricians agree to assist and provide follow-up in any way they can. They are relieved when they need to contact the neurosurgeon and receive a call back within the hour. They tell me that is a remarkable turnaround, almost unheard of. They understand first-hand the kind of quality care Evan is receiving across the country.

One-and-a-half years later, Randy's career moves us to a different region of the country. Continuity of care is vital in treating Apert syndrome—once you make a decision to go to a particular center you need to be prepared to stay with that center. So after all of our deliberations we would have had to travel somewhere anyway.

You are living an extraordinary life now—one that requires extraordinary measures. Do not let fear or doubt hold you back from doing your research and getting a second opinion. Getting a second opinion is a necessity and it is accepted as a normal course of action.

Nurses

Nurses are the heart and soul of the hospital. Every step of the way there have been nurses caring for Evan and making his quality of life the best it can be under the worst of circumstances.

Nurses generally work in eight or twelve-hour shifts. Before beginning a shift the nurse studies the patients' charts and has a meeting with the patients' current nurse. Nurses are amazing in their ability to be assigned a new patient and continue treatment seamlessly. The charge nurse assigns the nurses to the patients; you cannot choose who your nurse will be.

It is remarkable that in all the hundreds of wonderful nurses who have cared for Evan, we have only had one that didn't meet his needs. After unsuccessfully trying to work with the nurse to solve the problems, we spoke with the charge nurse. The end result was that we weren't assigned this nurse again.

Learn all that you can from the nurses that work with your child. When you see a particular technique that would be helpful to know, ask the nurse to give you a lesson. These skilled caregivers can teach you what you need to know in preparation for when it is time to take over completely at home.

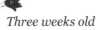

Three weeks old

Together, Evan's nurse and I change his bedclothes. She shows me how to make a nest in his bed by tightly rolling a blanket into a log and then placing it on his fresh bed in a U. Evan's bottom is snug to the bottom of the U, with the backs of his legs resting over the bottom of the U. She explains that the U nest will keep Evan more in one place. He will move around less and that will help keep all his wires and tubes fairly stationary. Another good thing about the U nest is that babies like to be snuggled in, feeling the firmness of their surroundings. It helps to make them feel secure.

The nurse says, "When he is crying and upset, try cupping your hand around his bottom and hold him firmly. Try nestling a blanket right up under his legs and around to his back. It's the same idea. Babies love to feel snug and secure."

Feeding Specialist

A feeding specialist may work with you to figure out the complexities of your child's nutritional needs. For Evan, this meant overcoming his struggles with a cleft palate and digestive issues. For us, this meant endless trial and error with bottles, formulas, food thickeners, and medications.

Evan was removed from the NG tube when he was three weeks old. Because of the nature of his cleft palate, he couldn't create the suction needed to breastfeed. We tried standard bottles, a pigeon bottle, and finally we found success with a Habermann bottle. A Habermann has a long nipple that is squeezed, pushing the milk into the baby's mouth. I learned to gently massage his jaw and move his chin up and down, encouraging him to swallow, while alternately squeezing the nipple, all with one hand.

For six weeks I was able to pump breast milk. However, pumping was time consuming and exhausting. The process started to spiral downward with less to show for it each day despite my best efforts.

Six weeks old

I am discouraged because I can't produce enough milk for Evan. It seems like the least I could do for him is to give him this one advantage—the best nutrition possible. I can't give up trying, even though my body isn't cooperating and pumping just isn't working. By the time I finish pumping, it is time to start feeding Evan again. By the time I finish feeding him, it is time to start pumping again. The slow agonizing process continues endlessly.

My brother-in-law, a nurse, takes me aside and says, "This is a situation where you need to think of the airplane image. You know, where the flight attendant says, 'If you have small children and there is an emergency, put an air mask on you first and then help your child.' You won't be any good to Evan if you don't take of yourself. Lots and lots of people have to feed their babies formula. It's really going to be fine if you just go completely to formula. You can't do everything. You have a lot of other important work that you have to do and you have to take care of yourself in order to do all that important work. You got in six weeks—that's great. It is perfectly okay to give up pumping now."

I decide to save myself in order to save Evan, and I put the pump in the back of a closet and walk away. I begin a new, energized routine, free of the pump and thankful for my extra time.

Research says that breast milk is the best for babies. But when you have a special needs child, sometimes you have to make decisions that are less than perfect. That is simply reality. Always take care of yourself in order to take care of your child.

After switching completely to formula, Evan developed digestive issues. We tried many different formulas and ended up with a soy formula that was the easiest for him to digest. Another possible option to investigate (one I was not aware of myself at the time, but has been active since 2006) is the National Milk Bank, found at the website: http://www.nationalmilkbank.org.

We discovered that using food thickeners in the formula (baby cereal or commercially made powder and gel thickeners) made it easier for Evan to swallow and keep the liquids down.

To minimize reflux, we found mixed results using a combination of different strategies: soy formula, food thickeners, reflux medication, simethicone drops, and lots of time massaging and burping Evan. Around three years of age we were able to eliminate all of these routines. One word of caution: be vigilant about the possible side effects of any medication you give for reflux. We found the flora in Evan's digestive system to be extremely sensitive to these medications. Read information pamphlets included with the medications carefully and be on alert.

Finally, at twelve months old, Evan began using a Soft Sip bottle by Zip-N-Squeeze for liquids. It is a soft bottle with flexible straw—a great tool for patients recovering from mouth surgery and young children learning how to suck from a straw. I probably could have started this system much sooner, had I been aware of it. At this time we also introduced soft foods using mesh food bags that he could suck on. As his diet became more varied, we added in daily probiotics.

It has been a time consuming and exhausting process, but feeding Evan gets a little easier every day. Seven years later, Evan is still a slow eater and mostly needs soft food. But he is a steady eater and enjoys good food enthusiastically.

Child Life Specialists

Child Life specialists are experts on the developmental needs of children during a hospital stay and the resources that are available to your child in the hospital. Here you can find the answers to questions like:

- How should I be stimulating my child's cognitive development?
- What kinds of toys and books are available in the hospital?
- What kinds of music would soothe and enrich my child?
- Are there CD players and CDs available in the hospital?
- What are some ideas for interaction I can have with my child at this stage of development?
- What can I do to comfort my frightened child?

Child Life specialists run playrooms and plan activities for older children who are able to move around and need the stimulation of new surroundings away from their hospital room. Child Life specialists also bring toys, books, CDs, and movies to children who are restricted to their rooms.

You can request to meet with the Child Life specialist to see what is available in your hospital. Take advantage of this resource and find some new ideas about how to meet your child's developmental needs while in the hospital.

Social Workers

A social worker can be a valuable resource in navigating through healthcare systems and community programs.

The social worker assisted us in enrolling Evan to receive Medicaid for the first few months he was in the hospital. She taught us the best ways to navigate our private insurance, which included signing up for a care coordinator who we contacted for all of our insurance questions.

Some families may be eligible for a variety of benefits while in the hospital. For those struggling financially, as many parents do during a health crisis, it is helpful to ask to speak with the social worker or patient advocate. A simple way to start a conversation: "We were caught totally unprepared for this health crisis. We are struggling financially. Do you know of any assistance that might be available for us while we are in the hospital? We would be grateful for any help."

The social worker may have access to other types of assistance:

- Special events and meals for family members
- Food vouchers, parking passes, phone cards
- Sleep rooms for parents caught unexpectedly without overnight accommodations
- Referral application to stay at a Ronald McDonald House

The social worker assisted us with our transition from the hospital. She coordinated the services that were necessary and available for Evan once he was situated at home. Some helpful services in my state included the *Birth to Three Program*, which oversees services for special needs children until they reach age three. At age three, services are turned over to the public school domain. Each family must begin to learn about any public or private services available in their own geographic area.

Spiritual Services

Consider meeting with the hospital chaplain (may include a minister, rabbi, priest, or other specially trained clergy member) when you need someone objective, knowledgeable, and inspiring to talk to. I discovered that hospital chaplains are some of the best-trained counselors around. They are knowledgeable in hospital life and can offer lots of insight about how to cope in the hospital. They are experienced in caring for people in pain and they can offer comfort. They have an unparalleled depth of empathy and are excellent listeners. You don't have to be affiliated with a church to see a spiritual services counselor. They are there for everyone and they understand that spirituality is expressed in many different ways.

Four days old

A hospital chaplain stops to visit us. She marvels at Evan's personality, already sweet and captivating. We are at ease with her—steadied by her calm presence and gentle warmth that fills the space around all of us. The next day she visits again. I tell her about Apert syndrome and the surgeries that Evan will need. She understands the struggles we are facing as we try to navigate through this new life we have been dropped into. She suggests hospital resources we didn't know about.

Later, I am alone and receive troubling news about Evan's health. Needing somebody to talk with, I ask for the chaplain. She sits with me, listens, understands, and offers bits of hope and wisdom. I have in her a confidante who knows through experience and training how to soothe my soul when hope is hard to find. She does not recite doctrine, but upon my request she eloquently offers a prayer.

If you have questions and need a neutral, competent counselor to talk with about your fears, a chaplain might be the person who could help you the most. You could gain new ideas and a new perspective.

four

UNDERSTANDING
INSURANCE

Medical Bills and Insurance

Four weeks old

We are inundated with paperwork and we begin to feel the financial impact of all the medical care. One month of hospital stays, doctor's bills, and laboratory tests have generated more invoices than we could have ever imagined. I pick up one bill from the hospital and open it. Is it possible that this invoice is for ninety thousand dollars and it only covers a few days of being in the hospital?

I try to guess what our share of this bill will be. It doesn't look like insurance has paid anything on it yet. The amount that we are left with could be devastating. But I don't know what our share will add up to, because I don't know what our health insurance will cover. I pull out all the medical bills and put them in a pile. Then I pull out all the letters from the insurance company and put them in a separate pile. I find our health insurance policy and put it on top of the piles. That is enough for now.

Understanding Your Insurance Benefits

If you are fortunate enough to be among those who have health insurance, I encourage you to read your health insurance policy carefully. Understand that what you have is a contract between you and an insurance company. With this contract you have agreed to pay a certain premium and in return you are eligible to receive certain benefits.

I have expended countless hours and considerable emotional energy working with insurance companies. Many of my experiences thinking about insurance and working with insurance companies have left me emotionally exhausted. I know firsthand that health insurance plays a crucial part in caring for a medically fragile child. In order to present the most helpful and accurate information possible, I consulted with a health insurance professional who has worked in the industry for more than twenty years and has a passion to help parents like you and me better understand our health insurance. My goal is to help alleviate some of the emotional turmoil we all experience when we are thrust into this system with no prior knowledge. The learning process can be excruciating, confusing, and financially devastating. But understanding the facts sooner than later can make everything much easier.

What I'm about to say next most likely will not feel good to read and it may not seem fair; it may make you angry. I have gone through all these emotions, and I understand them well. But after years of working with insurance companies in order to receive benefits, I know this to be true. Additionally, our health insurance professional wants you to know this. Here goes....

You may be thinking: "I have been paying all this money to an insurance company and now the time has come when I need benefits, therefore I am entitled to have all my expenses paid in full. Otherwise, why would I have been paying all this money all along?"

Unfortunately this is not the case. You are entitled to *some* benefits, according to the contract you signed with your insurance company. Depending on the terms of your policy and the contract you signed, you may be entitled to a lot of benefits. Or you may be entitled to fewer benefits. The cold hard truth is that you have entered into a contractual agreement and you are responsible for knowing all the terms of the policy you signed onto. That means you are responsible for knowing what benefits you are entitled to receive and what portion of the expenses you will be required to pay out of pocket. It is not the insurance company's responsibility to guide you through each healthcare decision you make in order to ensure that your expenses will be paid correctly. You signed a contract and it is your responsibility to know what is in it before you accept any medical services.

It isn't fair that parents of medically fragile children are left to deal with expenses that most people won't ever have. The fact that one healthcare crisis can seriously devastate the financial health of a family is one of the most painful truths in healthcare today. However, it is quite possible that your child may be eligible for some public assistance healthcare programs. If this turns out to be the case, some degree of fairness could be restored to your financial burden.

Terminology

Until we had Evan, we had no reason to understand the fine print details of our insurance policy. Our family had been very healthy and we rarely went to see doctors. Now we find ourselves needing to know every term and exactly how the carefully worded clauses will affect whether our medical bills will be paid or not. I would suggest that you learn all the terms used by your insurance company as soon as possible. Read your policy or go online to browse your insurance company's website for a glossary and additional valuable information and online services.

To get you started, here are some of the essential terms to look for in your policy. These terms are provided to help you know what to look for as you begin the process of understanding your own health insurance policy. These terms are by no means all inclusive and the definitions may change from policy to policy. Again, it is your responsibility to know what is in the contract you signed and the terms you agreed to when you signed up for your health insurance.

Insurance Terms Glossary

- **Coinsurance (sometimes referred to as coins):** The amount you are responsible for after your deductible is met. It is usually defined as a percentage with a maximum out-of-pocket amount. For example, a policy might state it this way: twenty percent of all expenses up to a $2,000 maximum out of pocket. Every policy is different.

- **Copay:** A fixed dollar amount paid each time you visit a doctor or have a hospital stay or have other specified expenditures (for example, prescriptions). Copayments apply even after deductible and coinsurance requirements are met. Every policy is different.

- **Deductible:** Upfront out-of-pocket cost, usually a set dollar amount, which must be paid prior to receiving any other benefits from insurance. Within a family, understand if each person needs to meet a deductible amount or if there is one amount for the entire family.

- **Explanation of Benefits (EOB):** A document provided by the insurance company that summarizes how benefits of your plan were applied to a specific claim. EOBs include date of service (DOS), discounted amount (if there is a discount contract that has been negotiated with the provider), coinsurance amount (if applicable), deductible (if applicable), and amount paid by insurance. The amount you are responsible for paying may also be stated.

- **In-network:** Healthcare providers and services that are covered under your insurance plan.

- **Out-of-network:** Healthcare providers and services that are not covered under your insurance plan.

- **Out-of-pocket Maximum:** the most you would expect to pay for medical expenses for the plan year.

- **Preauthorization:** Provided by the insurance company for specific procedures in order for benefits to be applied.

- **Precertification:** Authorization by the insurance company for non-emergency (predetermined) procedure or hospital stay. Often precertification must be completed by a specified period before the procedure or hospital stay in order to obtain insurance benefits.

- **Preferred Care Provider (PCP):** The healthcare providers that are considered "in-network" in your policy.

- **Provider:** Doctors or facilities that provide the healthcare service.

Conditions of Your Insurance Plan

As you read through your insurance policy, here are some of the questions to ask and the answers to search for:

- Does your plan require you to see certain providers? If so, which providers do you need to see?

- Are your benefits different for in-network versus out-of-network providers?

- Do you pay a copay to see a doctor? Do you pay a different copay to see a specialist?

- Are there any penalties to go to the ER instead of calling a preferred care provider?

- Is there a copay to go to the ER or urgent care center? If so, what is it?

- Are there any benefit limitations? (For instance, a certain number of visits, or dollar cap per plan year for specific services.)

- Are any services limited or excluded? (Check age limitations, cosmetic procedures, out-of-country exclusions.)

- Can you see an out-of-network provider and still receive benefits? What are the benefits (often paid at a lower rate)? What do you need to do in order to see an out-of-network provider?

- Is a referral required to see an out-of-network provider? How do you obtain one? Does it need preapproval?

- Does a hospital stay require precertification? If so, what is the protocol? If you're hospitalized on an emergency basis, do you still need to get the stay certified? In what timeframe?

- Can you file an appeal? What information is needed? When can you appeal? Does the appeal need to be made in a certain timeframe? What is the timeframe?

- Is a second surgical opinion ever required? When? (A second surgical opinion is something that insurance can request to decide if a procedure is required and is a procedure that will be eligible to receive benefits.)

Explanation of Benefits

An Explanation of Benefits (EOB) is issued for each medical provider claim. Every time you see a doctor or have a laboratory test, the bill (a claim) is sent to your insurance company. The insurance company determines what amount they pay and what amount you are responsible to pay, based on the benefits of your plan. Insurance sends payment to the medical provider and sends you an EOB. After the medical provider applies the insurance payment to the claim, you will be sent a bill for any remaining amount that you are responsible for.

Study the EOB until you understand the information it contains. There will be a description of the medical claim and the date of service. Look for the amount that has been paid on the medical claim by insurance and then look for any remaining amount that you are responsible for.

If the amount that you are responsible for is $0 (zero), breathe a sigh of relief and keep the material in a file for easy access if needed (suggested file heading: EOB—current year—paid in full).

If there is an amount due that you are responsible for and you know that you are responsible for paying it, place that bill with your unpaid medical bills.

If there is an amount due that you are responsible for and you feel that it is an error, verify that the claim was paid accurately. Look in your policy and review your benefits. Call your insurance case manager to confirm that the claim was paid correctly. If you think that you are entitled to a benefit, and the insurance company determines differently, you have the right to file an appeal within a specific timeframe.

You may only have a very short time to file your appeal. Appeals filed after the allowable time period designated by your insurance company may be automatically denied. Look in your policy and find the appeals timeline, the proper procedures, and the necessary paperwork. Gather everything you need, and complete all required paperwork. Send everything by certified mail in order to have a record of the day the insurance company receives the appeal; this will prove whether you filed your appeal within the time period designated by the insurance company. Remember to make your own personal copies of everything that you are mailing in and keep all of this information together in a file.

Now you must wait for a formal response. During this time contact the medical provider and explain that you have filed an appeal with the insurance company. Request to delay making payments (or arrange a small monthly payment) until the appeal process is complete.

Is This a Part-time Job?

At this point you may be thinking to yourself that doing all the business tasks that need to be done is equal to having a part-time job. It is. It takes specialized skills: terminology understanding, basic math ability (at least a good calculator), organizational flair, and finesse in communicating with various healthcare entities. And, while you do not earn a salary, the money you are spending and saving by following through correctly can be thought of as a salary in and of itself.

Rather than wallow in self-pity, fear, and/or procrastination at this work, I try to put myself in the mindset as if I am going to work. I am working for our family in order to keep the business end of our healthcare needs under control. Every bit of energy I put into this helps my family remain financially solvent. This positive spin empowers me and gives me the inspiration I need to face challenges head on.

One of the first steps in empowering yourself in this new "career" is to set up an effective file system that you will use. Here is the file system that I have developed that keeps me on track.

- **Appointment Cards:** I write the appointment on the calendar and save all the appointment cards here.

- **After Visit Summaries:** I place all discharge papers and summaries here for quick reference.

- **In Box—New Healthcare Bills, EOBs, and Precertifications:** I put all the incoming healthcare papers in here. When I have received both the bill and the EOB (and precertification or preauthorization as provided) I staple them together and move the packet to one of the following three files:

- **Medical Bills—Questions:** Unpaid bill with EOB and a blank piece of paper on top—stapled together. The blank paper is for notes from the necessary follow-up calls.

- **Medical Bills—To Pay:** All unpaid bills with EOBs go in this file. This includes physician and hospital bills, medical equipment, and all other miscellaneous expenses related to healthcare (except prescriptions).

- **Medical Bills—Finished:** All paid bills with matching EOBs go in this file.

- **EOBs—Paid in Full:** Any EOBs that indicate a medical bill has been paid in full are filed in here.

- **Prescriptions:** I save all receipts.

- **Health Insurance Information:** Policy and all notices go in here.

- **Flex Plan:** Information and forms.

- **Flex Plan—to Submit:** Collected and saved detailed invoices that include each procedure's complete description (a credit card receipt is not acceptable).

- **Flex Plan—Finished Claims:** Copies of all the claims filed.

Getting the files set up and using them are the first steps. The next step is to follow-up regularly—even daily if needed—and keep progressing on the files that need work: make the follow-up calls regarding any questions you have, pay the bills you need to pay (if you can't pay them, move them to the questions file and make a payment plan), and submit the Flex or HSA claims.

Talking to Your Insurance Company

Every time you call the insurance company, have beside you the packet of medical bills and any EOB (with blank paper stapled on top) that you have questions about. Write down the date and time of the conversation, the full name of the representative, and detailed notes about what was discussed and what you were told.

Listen carefully. Don't just listen for what you want to hear. Listen for what you need to know. When you think you have the answers you need, restate the information to ensure your full understanding of what you have been told.

When you are done, ask if there is a reference number associated with this call. These notes are extremely important as you make arrangements for all of your child's health needs.

Many insurance companies offer a program that provides case managers (sometimes called care coordinators) for patients with ongoing complex health needs. Case managers, many of whom are nurses, will understand the issues you are facing and the terminology you use. These programs are generally beneficial to both you and the insurance company.

For the customer, case management provides a go-to person you may contact directly with questions, concerns, and insurance needs. It provides a single point of contact at the insurance company, rather than a random representative. This point of contact is familiar with your child's medical history. The personalized service will likely cut your time and frustration to a fraction of what it could have been.

For the insurance company, this program carefully monitors your choices for your child's treatment and maintains some degree of cost control. Case managers help the consumer make educated and informed decisions. They build a relationship with the consumer and help to prevent misunderstandings before they happen, regarding benefits. However, never forget that this person works for the insurance company. As much as they truly want to help you and advocate for what your child may need, ultimately they must follow the guidelines set forth by the insurance company and the policy that you carry.

Usual and Customary

In the event that you have to file an appeal with your insurance company, there are a few additional terms you may encounter:

- **Usual and Customary**—The National Association of Insurance Commissioners (NAIC) studies the entire country to determine the going rate for healthcare services. The going rates vary in different regions of the country. To determine the usual and customary fee for a region, many factors are taken into consideration, including average medical provider charges, average income of the entire population, and cost of living. In many cases insurance companies pay a percentage of the usual and customary fee.

- **CPT Code (current procedural terminology)**—These are codes that are developed by the American Medical Association to uniformly describe every medical procedure.

These terms are used to describe how your benefits were applied to the medical bill in question.

I appealed an insurance payment in one instance. It involved a payment to a medical provider who was out of state and was out of network with my insurance company. Over time I learned that bills are paid based on a formula that takes into consideration usual and customary fees for my geographical region based on the universal CPT codes.

It gets complicated when you have to travel out of state for treatment to a place where the usual and customary fees are higher than those where you live. Typically you are traveling to a larger metropolitan area where the usual and customary fees are higher than smaller or rural areas where you may live. This could have a dramatic effect on how much is actually paid to the medical provider in comparison to what the fee is. If you are seeing a provider who is not in-network with your insurance company, you may end up with a sizeable balance that you will be expected to pay.

Through the appeal process I was able to obtain an additional payment for the medical provider, but not the entire balance of the bill. The remaining balance was partially paid off over time through a payment plan and eventually was graciously written off by the medical provider.

Medical Bills

As painful as it might be, I encourage you to open medical bills as soon as you receive them. If it is really difficult for you to deal with, remember that you don't have to take action immediately, simply look for any red flags that you will have to address in the future and file in one of the Medical Bill files (Questions file, To Pay file, or Finished file).

Look to make sure that the claim has been submitted to insurance. If you get a medical bill before insurance has paid on the claim, it should say "insurance pending," "do not pay," or something similar. You must wait until insurance pays on the claim to know if you will be responsible for any balance. Watch for the EOB to arrive (either in the mail or electronically) for this claim.

I have had rare instances when a medical claim was submitted incorrectly to insurance, or submitted to the wrong insurance company, or not submitted at all. In these cases, I call the medical provider to verify the insurance information they have on file. Remember that some medical billing offices have to deal with many different insurance companies and mistakes can happen.

If there is a discrepancy between a medical bill and your EOB for the same claim, call your case manager. Try to gather information on the claim and sort out the issue with your case manager first, and then with the medical provider if necessary.

If you have a provider bill that you are responsible for and you can't pay the entire balance immediately, call the medical provider and arrange a payment plan. In some instances of financial hardship and the right timing for the medical provider, you can reach an agreement in which part or all of the balance is written off or forgiven on the medical provider's year-end expenses.

COBRA Continuation of Health Coverage

COBRA (Consolidate Omnibus Budget Reconciliation Act) is an important program to understand if you are leaving an employed position or switching insurance companies. COBRA is a federally regulated program (Department of Labor) that allows those who participate in an employer health plan in a company with twenty or more employees to continue their insurance coverage if their employment situation changes (loss of employment, disability, relocation, layoff). The cost of COBRA is expensive, but it allows continuity of benefits for a period of eighteen months. Extension of benefits can be applied to medical, dental, vision, and flexible spending plans.

This is important to consider, especially when preexisting conditions are present. Currently insurance companies can exclude treatment on preexisting conditions when health insurance is started after a period of sixty days of being uninsured. COBRA can serve as the bridge that prevents any lapse of insurance that would put you at risk for having payment denied for treatment of preexisting conditions.

If an individual doesn't qualify for COBRA (their plan is not through an employer with twenty or more employees), there is a "state continuation" requirement. The details of these plans vary from state to state. Find more information by contacting your state's Department of Insurance.

Flexible Spending Account

Flexible Spending Accounts (FSA) and Healthcare Savings Accounts (HSA) are valuable tools to consider utilizing. The income used to pay into these accounts is not taxed and these accounts provide a way to save money for healthcare expenses. However, you must carefully project how much money you will use each year. With some FSA/HSAs, any money that is placed in an account and not used within the year will be lost.

These programs are regulated by the IRS. The IRS dictates what is and isn't covered under these programs. You must save and provide all receipts for healthcare expenses when participating in these programs in accordance with IRS regulations.

Assistance Programs

Public Assistance programs and public healthcare options vary from state to state, are usually in transition, and usually have limited funding. Assistance funding comes primarily from federal sources and is then allocated to state and county programs.

To be eligible for programs, a child may have to meet certain level of care requirements. The parents will have to document the activities of daily life (ADL) that their child requires assistance with.

For a newborn, this can be challenging to prove. Newborns need assistance with all areas of living. In order to qualify for assistance, a child may require hospitalization or a level of in-home skilled nursing that other newborns don't require. Examples of skilled nursing might include giving tracheostomy care, feeding tube maintenance, or intense respiratory care. While medically fragile children require intense caregiving, they may not require skilled nursing care. It can be discouraging to discover that your child may not qualify for some types of assistance, especially when other parents appear to be floating through a normal family life and you may be struggling to meet your child's complex health needs.

As a child gets older, he may begin to meet more of the requirements for assistance with ADL. Take walking as an example. Newborns can't walk, so this doesn't count as a qualification for assistance with activities of daily life. However, according to the American Academy of Pediatrics, the developmental milestone for walking is usually met by the age of two. If a child isn't walking by age two, this can be used to formulate a case that the child needs assistance.

I have found the American Academy of Pediatrics book, *The Complete and Authoritative Guide, Caring for your Baby and Young Child*, very helpful in assessing my child's development. It contains guidelines for developmental milestones (movement, hand and finger skills, language, cognitive, and social) that are normally reached by specific ages. When filling out applications to receive assistance, it may be beneficial to quote milestones outlined in this book that your child hasn't met and give reference to the book.

Another source to refer to in assessing typical development milestones is the National Dissemination Center for Children with Disabilities: www.nichcy.org/disability/milestones.

A search for state and county assistance can begin on the Internet. Seek out state and county government websites and look for *Health and Human Services* and *Child and Family Services*. Every state and county implements programs uniquely. At this time, there isn't any one program or process that uniformly serves all children with special healthcare needs throughout the country.

Representation and Guidance

If you have problems obtaining benefits or service from your insurance company, go to the website of the Department of Insurance for your state. You will find company information, complaint forms and reports, glossary of terms, and contact information.

There are nonprofit legal agencies that advocate for disabled individuals. These organizations have experience in how to formulate and assemble complaints, appeals, and assistance applications. To find an agency that serves your state, try a search using keywords such as "health and disability advocates" or "advocacy and benefits counseling for health". Or, contact a special healthcare needs agency in your state and ask for names of nonprofit advocacy or legal organizations they recommend.

SKILLS

More Capable

One year old

The challenges we face are forcing us to become more resourceful and more capable. With each experience we hone new skills: confidence, advocacy, observation, intuitive thinking, organization. We discover that even being happy is a skill, one that takes intent and determination.

We are empowered as parents and in all parts of our lives. We develop a deeper understanding of the human condition and what it means to live a life with responsibility and meaning. None of this personal growth would have been possible had we not been given the life that we have with Evan.

Have Confidence in What You Know

We knew the baby basics—swaddling a newborn, changing diapers, giving bottles, and singing lullabies. We had experienced the weird but normal things that babies do which shoot panic through a new parent's veins. Things like when babies make weird sounds as they discover their voice, when they projectile vomit with no warning, when they expel what we call "nuclear burps," or when they roll their eyes back, showing the whites of their eyes (like a character in a horror movie) as they learn how to work their eye muscles. You can really only understand these strange and wonderful milestones if you have seen them.

Three weeks old

Evan's nurse meets us as we arrive at his room. Obviously delivering some serious news, we brace ourselves. She tells us that the intern on duty last night saw Evan having seizures. He was vomiting and rolling his eyes back so only the whites were showing.

They are watching him closely now and he seems to be doing well. The treatment to prevent future seizures is a drug called phenobarbital, described to us as a medication that would need to be taken for a lifetime once started. That sounds ominous.

I can't recall seeing anything like a seizure when I have been with Evan.

He had been spitting up a lot. I hadn't noticed anything with his eyes, but I do remember Jonathan, as an infant, rolling his eyes back and how unsettling is was. I think about the intern who is young and probably hasn't ever experienced these weird but normal baby behaviors. In which case, it probably could have seemed like Evan was having a seizure, but maybe he wasn't.

A friend who is knowledgeable in this area cautions us to be very careful starting Evan on phenobarbital. It's a powerful drug and would probably mean a lifetime of depending on it. Not something to be started lightly. But if Evan does have a seizure disorder, then yes, this would be a beneficial and necessary drug. He suggests watching Evan closely—watch for seizures—but don't start any drug like phenobarbital without tests showing specific evidence of a seizure.

We ask for the tests and they came back negative. I watch Evan like a hawk—no seizures. So I am comfortable taking the "wait and see" approach. Not that I'm not on edge—I am. Time continues on, seizure free. We never start the drug and Evan has never needed it.

Do not disregard any information that a doctor gives you. This is a critical time and you need to make sure that your child receives the treatment he needs. But if you have questions or doubts, be very sure in your own mind that this is the right step. If you are given time to think about a decision, take it. Use the knowledge you have and find people who can offer more ideas. Get a second opinion. Make informed decisions and have confidence in what you know.

Be a Diplomatic Advocate

As a parent and a consumer of healthcare services, you have the right to share your ideas, to make requests, and to file complaints regarding your child's care. But think about how you can be most effective. List your concerns clearly (caregivers cannot read your mind and don't have time to guess what you are upset about), be diplomatic, and then wait. Give the person you are addressing time to understand your concerns, to think about what is best for the patient, and to offer possible solutions. Always do your part to maintain a positive relationship with the healthcare professionals.

Five weeks old

Our attention is drawn to Evan, not because he is moving about, but because he is still. Completely still. His eyes are open and staring blankly. We jump up, call to him, touch him. The monitor alarms begin to sound—his vital signs are dropping. I lift his upper body up and pat his back. His face turns red—where is the nurse? He blinks and takes a breath. His vital sign numbers return to normal. I press the call button for the nurse.

By the time she gets to our room, Evan seems normal. The moment of panic has passed and we are left alone again. But the scene replays itself over and over and we are left to deal with it mostly on our own. I fume and my patience is worn out. Why are we in the hospital if someone isn't going to come to the rescue when Evan stops breathing?

I make a list of all my concerns:

- Evan struggling with apnea for two hours.

- Oxygen saturations are dropping down below 85.

- He stops breathing completely.

- His monitors are going off and nobody is coming to check on him.

I call for the attending physician and share all of my concerns with him. I end by saying, "This floor seems very busy and the nurses seem to really have their hands full. Evan needs more constant care right now. I don't think this pediatric floor is the best place for him today. I think he needs to be monitored more closely and needs to be moved to the PICU." And then I wait. Silence is a powerful tool. I give him time to look at Evan's condition and to come up with a response.

The doctor agrees with me. Evan is moved to the PICU and he receives the care he needs.

To be an effective advocate, define your concerns in your own mind, make a clear request, and then give wait time for a response. The wait time is vital. It demands an action from whomever you are addressing.

- I am concerned that my child isn't being monitored closely enough. What is the schedule? Would there be any way to have a nurse come in more frequently? (Stop talking and wait for a response.)

- I am concerned that my child is still in pain. What could be done to help ease the pain, more than is already being done? (Stop talking and wait for a response.)

- I noticed that my child's bed is dirty. What is the schedule for changing the bed? I would feel better if it could be done more frequently (Stop talking and wait for a response.)

- I think that my child would be more comfortable if he were bathed more frequently. What is the schedule? (Stop talking and wait for a response).

- I feel _____, when _____ happens. Is there anything that could be done to fix this? (Stop talking and wait for a response.)

Go through the proper chain of command. First talk to your nurse. If you aren't satisfied with the results, then talk to the charge nurse. If you still aren't satisfied, then talk to the attending physician. If your problem still isn't resolved, then go to a hospital administrator or patient advocate. These caregivers are dedicated and do want the best for their patients. They are also busy and aren't able to be with the patient at all times. Sometimes you encounter a unit having a bad day—everyone has them. You, as the parent, are a vital part of the caregiver team and you must do your part to ensure that your child is getting everything he needs. At the same time, create a good working relationship with your child's caregiver team by expressing your concerns clearly, positively, and giving the opportunity to reach a satisfactory solution.

Share What You Know

You are the constant factor in your child's care. You know what is normal, and what is not normal. If you are concerned about a new symptom, speak up. A piece of information that you share might be the missing link to a complex problem.

Nine weeks old

We rush to the ER, still frustrated by these unexplained episodes of apnea. The ER physician steps into Evan's room and begins her evaluation. Listening to his heart she looks up and says, "That's quite a murmur he has," almost as if acknowledging a little pet he carries around with him.

"Murmur?" I am surprised. "Nobody has ever mentioned a murmur before."

She reassures me, "It's very common and nothing to worry about. Many babies develop a murmur as they get bigger."

"But this is strange," I insist. "His heart has been listened to almost every day for months. Nobody has ever said anything about a heart murmur."

Responding with confidence, the doctor says, "Really, it isn't anything to worry about. I'll go look over his chart and come back in a little while."

I am unconvinced and concerned. Surely someone would have said something before if Evan had a heart murmur. Nobody has ever mentioned it.

The doctor returns to our room. "You know, I hear something in your voice telling me that we need to take a closer look at this murmur. Let's do an echocardiogram, just to rule out anything out of the ordinary."

The test shows that it isn't an ordinary murmur. The left side of Evan's heart is significantly enlarged— apparently a side effect caused by a steroid he had started just two weeks earlier and was scheduled to be on for an extended time. He is rapidly tapered off of the steroid and within a month his heart returns to its normal size.

I shudder to think what could have happened if we hadn't discovered his heart condition that night. Always remember that you hold important information about your child. You cannot be shy about sharing what you know and initiating discussions. Doctors know what is normal for the *general* population, but they do not always know specifically what is normal for *your child*.

Trust your Intuition

There are times when you need to let your instincts and intuition lead you. A parent's instincts are powerful—listen to yours.

Ten weeks old

Evan's apnea continues to be perplexing. It is a frightening cycle that has continued for months: his eyes become fixed, his body becomes still, his face turns reddish blue. We call his name, pat him, give him oxygen, and pray for him to breathe.

Different doctors have different theories: an obstruction in his throat, a malfunction with his heart or lungs, a neurological problem, an allergic reaction. Nobody can determine the exact cause. I start to notice a pattern that the apnea usually begins after he eats and I begin to develop my own theory. Could it be that he has gas bubbles that are getting trapped and he just isn't strong enough to move them?

I share my thoughts with the attending hospital physician and ask, "Could we give Evan those drops for babies that relieve gas bubbles?"

The doctor looks skeptical and answers, "Well, those drops are really just for colicky babies who cry a lot and can't be consoled. Evan isn't colicky. I really don't think that it would help—he doesn't need them."

I feel silly for asking the doctor and I don't press him any further.

A few days later, I tell a friend about my idea. She has babies of her own who have colic and she swears by the drops (generic name, smithecone). She doesn't have any idea if they would help Evan, but she says that they have really helped her kids.

Two weeks later, during a time at home, Evan still struggles with apnea and the cycle starts again. By chance, this same friend is walking past our house. I yell out to her and she runs to get us some of the drops. I give them to Evan and miraculously he begins burping and starts breathing easily again.

We start a routine of giving Evan smithecone drops regularly with feedings. We perfect the best burping positions and massage his back—stroking upwards to bring the bubbles up. While he still struggles after eating, we now have a course of action to follow. Our challenges with apnea are over.

In retrospect, I should have persisted with the doctor when I first had the idea to try the drops. I should have asked him questions like:

- Is there any reason not to try this?

- Would there be any harm in trying this?

- Are there any dangerous side effects to this?

- I would like to try this, if it doesn't help could we try something else?

Listen to your instincts and let them guide you. Do not allow yourself to feel silly for asking a question or suggesting a solution that someone else hasn't thought of. Sometimes the simple answer is the right answer.

Stay Organized

Forewarned is forearmed: you are about to face mountains of paperwork. I am not exaggerating. You will be inundated with medical bills, EOBs (explanation of benefits from insurance companies), appointment cards, prescriptions, applications, notes, and much, much more. Expect it, prepare for it, organize it, and deal with it.

Tips to get you started

- If you have a smart phone or tablet, learn how to use the organizing tools.

- Keep your calendar with you at all times.

- Keep your notebook with you at all times.

- Set up three spots (I use baskets) for the incoming mail that you can't deal with immediately:
  - Medical bills
  - Insurance papers
  - Household bills

- Set up files to hold your papers:
  - Appointment Cards (Enter the appointment on your calendar and file the card)
  - After Visit Summaries
  - Prescription Receipts
  - Medical Bills—Questions
  - Medical Bills—To Pay
  - Medical Bills—Finished
  - EOBs—Paid in Full
  - Flex Plan—Information

- Flex Plan—To Submit

- Flex Plan—Finished Claims

- Health Insurance Information

- Additional files for information regarding specific health conditions (for example, asthma)

- Applications for Assistance—copy and save every application you fill out. (Chances are you will have to reapply yearly and you can refer back to the previous application you filled out. I find it helpful to make a note of how long it took me to fill out the application. That way next year I can be prepared to set aside the right amount of time.)

Stay ahead of the game. I know from experience that the times I have let my paperwork get out of control are no fun. The prospect of organizing and doing all that needs to be done is debilitating. It has the power to darken days and cause sleepless nights. So, be prepared. Have a place for everything and keep everything in its place.

Happiness

What brings you happiness? For some, happiness depends on things, other people, our place in society, or maybe our career. Do you evaluate each day; wait to see how things unfold? Or is happiness a state of existence, either you are or you aren't? Can it be a choice to let go of negativity and resistance and just be content?

Five years old

When I was pregnant with our first son, I prayed every night that he would be healthy. When I was pregnant with Evan I had many friends struggling with unhappy teenagers. I saw firsthand how difficult life is for an unhappy soul who is struggling to find his way. So then I prayed every night that Evan would be happy. As it turns out, he is the happiest person I know. He loves to smile, giggle, and say, "This is going to be so, so fun." It is truly wonderful to be around such happiness.

Every person who meets Evan is captivated by his happiness in life, despite all of his physical challenges. They are in turn inspired to rise up to his level of zeal for life, motivated to overcome challenges or set aside disgruntlements they are facing in their own lives. Every day I am thankful for the gifts of joy that Evan spreads from person to person.

I believe happiness is a choice. Every day we have choices. You have choices as you embark on this new life. You can choose to be all the things that create an inspired life. I have chosen to define my life with words like: positive, strong, creative, thankful, proactive, and reflective.

If we are lucky, our lives are happy ones with time spent doing the things we love. I am reminded of this over and over. Evan has taught me how to make just about everything fun, to celebrate often, and to delight in the chance to experience a new day.

CARING FOR YOURSELF

Stretched into New Dimensions

Three weeks old

My mind and body are being stretched into new dimensions of existence. I am pushed into extreme and bizarre situations every day. It is harder and harder to stay grounded and have faith that eventually life will become somewhat normal again.

Almost one month into this experience, I am living and running my life from a hospital. Instead of simply changing a diaper, I am changing a diaper around all kinds of wires and tubes. Instead of just picking up the baby and nursing him, I am assembling a complex bottle that has to be put together just so, with just the right ingredients, with just the right technique, and holding him without pulling out an IV. Instead of planning "Mommy and Me" gatherings, I am planning several weeks' worth of doctor's appointments and evaluations. Instead of going on a trip to the grocery store, I am going on a trip across the country to begin a series of complicated surgeries.

As much as I need to be aware of Evan's needs, I also need to be aware of my own needs. Because the only way I can continue this seemingly endless odyssey, is to take care of myself, too.

Pace Yourself

Set a sustainable pace for yourself. It's like running a marathon and you can never run fast enough, hard enough, or long enough to finish everything that needs doing. The reality is that every day you will leave some things unfinished—with more that you could have done, no matter how hard you have pushed yourself.

Five Weeks Old

Randy and I divide our time between home and the hospital (they are an hour apart). I spend a few hours in the morning with Jonathan and then drive an hour through a busy interstate highway under construction to be with Evan for the day. Then I take the white-knuckle drive back home to tuck Jonathan into bed. When I have a few free moments I tackle the mountains of paperwork and arrange the details of Evan's long-range treatment plan.

A relative watching the whirlwind of activity says to me, "Pace yourself."

I am irritated that he would even suggest this. I nod and say, "You're probably right." But I think to myself, That's easy for you to say. How can I pace myself? There is too much to do to slow down, even for just a moment to THINK about pacing myself.

I keep racing from one thing to the next, but in my mind I still hear his voice say, "Pace yourself." What does my life look like from his perspective? Is there some undeniable wisdom in his words?

I discover that pacing myself is part of my acceptance process: accepting a new priority of life activities; accepting the fact that I was dealt a challenging hand and some things are going to be left unfinished; accepting help when it is offered to me; accepting the fact that I have to conserve and refuel my own energy, so that I can keep going for the long haul; accepting that my new life is a work in progress.

Your child needs you—a steady, calm, guiding presence for a long time to come, not a flurry of activity that leaves you, the center of his universe, collapsing in a heap of exhaustion. After seven years, our race is still going and we couldn't have come this far without pacing ourselves.

Create a Routine

The daily routine that I learned to create for myself kept me moving forward with purpose and prevented me from falling into a state of despondency. Every night I would look in my calendar at the days ahead, schedule in activities, and make a to-do list. The knowledge that each new day brought us closer to stability was the inspiration that kept me going and kept me planning ahead.

My routine when Evan was an infant in the hospital:

6:00 a.m.	Speak with doctors doing rounds
7:00 a.m.	Drive home
8:00 a.m.	Shower and eat breakfast
9:00 a.m.	Spend time with two-year-old Jonathan
11:00 a.m.	Drive to hospital
12:00 p.m.	Feed and spend time with Evan, Have a snack
2:30 p.m.	Evan naps Take a walk. Do paper work/make phone calls/run an errand.
4:00 p.m.	Feed and spend time with Evan Have dinner
7:00 p.m.	Final feeding for Evan
8:00 p.m.	Evan sleeps Read, visit CarePages, phone home, finish paperwork, look at calendar. Sleep in hospital room with Evan.

Randy spent a lot of time with our two-year-old, and friends helped with childcare. This made it possible for me to spend as much time with Evan as possible.

Our routine changed and evolved with each stage of development. Not only does a routine help you, but it also helps others working with you know what to expect (nurses, your other children, your partner, etc.) from your time.

Prayer

Find comfort and strength in your spiritual beliefs.

Six weeks old

After being tucked away in Evan's hospital room for days, I am restless and walk to the gift shop. I need something good to read—something to lift my spirits. The title God's Psychiatry by Charles L. Allen (Ravel, 1997) draws my interest. My father was a psychiatrist. He was great at giving out golden tidbits of advice. Thinking of him brings back a memory of him telling me, "Babies will take on the emotions of their mother. If a mother is sad or depressed, a baby will sense this and also be sad. Always be positive and happy with your babies. It is very important."

I open the book and read Psalm 23 followed by this sentence: "The power of the Psalm lies in the fact that it represents a positive, hopeful, faith approach to life." The book, using and explaining Psalm 23's words and imagery, guides the reader to transform one's mind from being troubled to being peaceful. This sounds like something I could use right about now. I buy the book and take it back to Evan's room to read.

Psalm 23(KJV)
> The Lord is my shepherd: I shall not want.
> He maketh me to lie down in green pastures;
> He leadeth me beside the still waters.
> He restoreth my soul: he leadeth me in the paths of
> righteousness for his name's sake.
> Yea, though I walk through the valley of the shadow
> of death, I will fear no evil: for thou art with me; thy rod
> and thy staff they comfort me.
> Thou preparest a table before me in the presence of
> mine enemies: thou anointest my head with oil; my cup
> runneth over.
> Surely goodness and mercy shall follow me all the
> days of my life: and I will dwell in the house of the Lord forever.

I was familiar with the words and had appreciated their beauty. But I never really understood exactly what the words meant, and how they could comfort and strengthen me until I read this book. This quiet time spent reading and exploring my own faith and spirituality always brings me peace and connects me to my inner strength.

However you define your spirituality, study the teachings that bring you peace. Absorb the wisdom in the words. Apply the lessons to your own life. Allow this time to create a peaceful presence for yourself and your child.

Meditation

Meditation is a technique that can transform your mind. An essential part of meditation is deep breathing, which increases oxygen to the brain and helps in decision making. If you haven't meditated before, you could start by finding an audio recording to guide you through a simple meditation. There are meditation CDs available and you can find audio recordings and downloads on the Internet. Use a search with the words *free online meditation audio* to get started.

Or, try a very basic self-guided meditation.

- Find a quiet space.

- Sit still in any position that is comfortable.

- Close your eyes.

- Breathe slowly and deeply. Feel your breath, listen.

- As you breathe, imagine your breath reaching each of your body parts one by one: head, chest, arms, fingers, stomach, legs, feet.

- Imagine your favorite spot in nature and see yourself there.

- Breathe slowly and deeply.

- Imagine nature around you expanding to an infinite space.

- Continue breathing slowly and deeply.

When I visualize the infinite size of the universe, my mind is opened to unlimited possibilities for everything. Even within the limits of physical challenges.

Take a Daily Walk

Walking can heal your mind, body, and spirit.

Reasons to Take a Daily Walk

1. To go outside and smell the fresh air.

2. To soak in the sight of trees, flowers, architecture, new faces.

3. To get some exercise, which is said to get your blood flowing and increase your dopamine and serotonin.

4. To take a time out from the pressure of your role as parent.

5. To give yourself some solitude to center yourself.

6. It could be the one thing that saves your sanity.

Six weeks old

Everyone in this situation has their breaking points—moments when you feel your world is collapsing upon you. There seems to be no one to turn to and nowhere to go. The nonstop daily pressure of being a superhero parent (with no end in sight) is enough to break the strongest person. I can feel myself reaching this point. It feels as if I am simultaneously exploding and imploding and yet I can't cry—I can't release the enormity of emotions coming over me.

I walk away from Evan's hospital room, with no idea of where I am headed. I think that maybe I am really losing it this time and I find myself in a long line at a mental health crisis unit. There is absolutely no way my emotions can be contained in this line, in this dim, quiet, polite room. While a crisis unit is probably the most logical place to be, my body won't allow it.

I escape to the university's campus where I release my energy like a wound-up top. I break into a run, racing blindly and not noticing my surroundings—just pushing the emotion out of my body. Energy released, my pace slows and I start to see the trees, buildings, and flowers. I feel the warmth of the sun, breathe in the air, and listen to the birds. I sit on a bench and just breathe. I close my eyes and sit without thinking. I fade into the scene and rest. Then, hoping I remember where I came from, I slowly make my way back. I feel better. At least strong enough to slip back into Evan's room and return to my odd new world.

From that day forward, a walk becomes part of my daily routine. Taking my walk resets my emotions and my thoughts and gives me renewed energy.

My Garden

Continue doing whatever creative projects you love to do. It is part of who you are. Develop your creativity because it will inspire you, bring you joy, and always be one of your greatest assets.

Gardening is my creative passion. I love to work outside in nature, feeling the sun, breathing in the fresh air, digging in the soil, planting flowers, and listening to the wildlife. It nurtures my soul and feeds my imagination.

Seven weeks old

It is late summer now, August, and my cousin Penny has arrived from Wisconsin. She spends time with Jonathan at our home while we spend time with Evan at the hospital. Our southern climate has passed through the height of its sweltering heat, and it is bearable outside once again. Penny and Jonathan play in our yard, swinging, running, exploring. Penny, an avid gardener, can't help but notice that our yard doesn't have a flower garden. She has been drawn to the concept of therapy gardening and she is sure that a garden is just what I need.

And so we embark on our diversion, my first non-medical adventure since Evan was born. We set off for the farmer's market, leaving all the worries behind. My senses awaken at the sights and smells—vegetables, fruits, jams, cheeses, shrimp, crafts, and of course flowers—beautiful flowers and plants—gifts from Penny that will find a home in our yard.

Penny creates a garden map and we decide where to put all of our new gems. She has already prepared the plot and together we plant everything. I am struck by the deep richness of varied colors in our big patch of zinnias—cheerfully heralding the day. For the rest of my life my gardens must always have zinnias. Zinnias hold the memory of the day that I discovered great joy, even in our most troubled times.

After Penny leaves, I delight in caring for my garden. My eyes and hands anticipate the next brief moments that I will be able to water, weed, arrange rocks, and pick a bouquet. My neighbors tell me that they love to see me in my garden. It signals that my world is calm and that I am at peace, at least for the moment.

I continue to garden, always including zinnias. Gardening is the best healing therapy I know. The satisfaction of planting something beautiful, caring for it, watching it grow, and being in nature makes my heart happy.

Positive Affirmations

When doubt threatens to erode your resolve, know that there is tremendous power in positive thinking. Time and time again I have given myself the power to overcome hardships and challenges by thinking positive thoughts and saying positive affirmations. The secret to positive affirmations is that they get you thinking about what you have instead of what you don't have. Then your mind can lead your body to take action. A person's mind/body connection is powerful and needs to be harnessed during these difficult times. The more positive thinking you do, the more you are creating a positive reality.

Ten weeks old

I am scared that we won't have enough of almost everything I can think of. I feel a strong sense of deprivation—not enough sleep, not enough knowledge, not enough money, not enough joy, etc. This sense of deprivation and the negative conversation I have going with myself freezes my ability to take any kind of action. How can we survive with so little?

Since I have started sleeping in Evan's hospital room at night (three weeks into Evan's life), the "not enough" that I feel most deeply is "not enough sleep." My nights are filled with sporadic periods of sleep in between alarms going off, nurses coming and going, and Evan waking to be fed. I sleep fitfully on the little couch in the room. During the day I doze off as I pump milk, feed Evan, and wait for appointments. Today, right at this moment, I feel like I can't do one more thing until I have "enough sleep."

But I don't have time to sleep right now. So I begin to say to myself, "I have enough. I have enough energy for now. The energy of the Universe will keep me strong. God will give me whatever strength I need. I have enough." And I begin to have renewed energy. I move onward with the next action that needs to be done. I can keep going until the next time I am able to sleep. Whenever I say to myself, "I have enough"—I find that I really do have enough.

Choose short affirming phrases to repeat that will instantly give you strength and take away your fears.

Positive affirmations to try:

- I have enough.
- In this moment, right now, everything is okay.
- I can do anything that I need to do.
- I am watching and learning and becoming a skilled caregiver.
- I am strong and in control.

Do a Puzzle

I have learned to always have a crossword puzzle or Sudoku on hand. These types of mental challenges require the focused attention of my entire brain. To complete the puzzle, I have to put aside my worries for the moment, which is exactly what we all need from time to time. I especially like to do a puzzle before going to bed; my mind is released from the worries of the day.

Laugh

Let yourself laugh—regularly. Laughing at anything might feel wrong after all you've been through. With all the weighty matters looming, it probably doesn't seem right to laugh. It doesn't feel authentic because it doesn't reflect how you feel. But laughter is more than creating a sound reaction to something amusing. Recent scientific research is showing that laughing has a physiological impact on your body. Laughter stimulates the production of endorphins and human growth hormone (which boosts immunity). It also impacts blood vessels, allowing an increase in the flow of blood (which helps your heart).

Take a friend or your partner and create a cache of funny treasures—funny movies, books, CDs, comics. Try sending out an email to friends, requesting that they loan you their favorite funny entertainment. People love sharing what they got a good laugh from—it is human nature. When you are able to, lose yourself in one of your finds and laugh as much as you can.

Have a Thankful Attitude

A counselor shared a very useful technique with me during this time of challenges and not much good news. She suggested that at the end of the day I find three positive things to say. It can be anything. Just find three positive things to say—even though it can be tough to be thankful in the middle of a crisis.

At first, I had to really work to find what I was thankful for (a peaceful day, an easy feeding, a positive and energized nurse, an inspiring passage in a book, finishing one important task). But soon I began noticing more and more good things throughout the day that I was thankful for.

Learning to be thankful has reset my attitude and created an overall sense of positive energy. I know that if I am only ever talking about the problems in my day, I am creating a negative reality for myself. When I talk about the successes in my day, I am creating a positive reality for myself. This is one of the most important strategies I use to keep going day in and day out.

seven

IN-HOME
STRATEGIES

Going Home

Four weeks old

At last we are going home. Evan is strong enough to leave the hospital. We are elated. Jonathan will have his mommy and daddy together again. We will have our beds, our showers, our clothes, and our food. We will have our lives back. Sort of.

Our euphoria is tempered by the knowledge that now we alone are solely responsible for keeping Evan alive. We are shedding the safety nets of nurses, doctors, monitors, alarms, and medical equipment that have been close at hand, ready for the next emergency.

We put Evan in the car. I sit in the backseat with him and watch his every breath. Our trip home starts a vigil that will go on for years.

We learn how to survive being vigilant day and night. We learn how to discern true emergencies that require an ambulance to the hospital from difficult situations that we can manage at home. We begin to build a new life that is carefully crafted around meeting all of Evan's complex needs, while still longing to do normal family activities and routines like everyone else we know.

Our first trip home lasts eight days before apnea sends us back to the hospital via ambulance. This is the first of many terrifying emergencies we face at home. We return to the hospital frequently during Evan's first few years of life, making the times at home seem fleeting and dreamlike.

The first few years of Evan's life are a continuous cycle of hospital stays, doctor's appointments, pharmacy runs, therapy sessions, and surgeries. At the same time we are in a continual mode of caregiving: feeding, giving respiratory therapy, maintaining digestive issues, administering medicines, continuing all the therapy that Evan needs to grow stronger. Between this running around and caregiving we squeeze in all the mandatory paperwork and phone calls.

What Ifs

Self-doubt can be your worst enemy as you take over your child's care at home. When we brought Evan home we were responsible for a complex feeding routine, open sore care, changing the dressing on Evan's PICC line (peripherally inserted central catheter), continuous breathing treatments, and nighttime oxygen monitoring equipment. And this was just the beginning. Over time we have been faced with all sorts of nursing tasks that we were completely unfamiliar with. Naturally, at times we have questioned our abilities to do everything correctly. What if we make a mistake? What if we accidentally hurt our child?

The way I have overcome my own self-doubt is with preparation. I carefully study all the information I can find, ask questions, and practice with a nurse's supervision. Then, I just have faith in my abilities and do what needs to be done.

Seven weeks old

In our living room, Randy and I set up a sterile area and carefully lay out all of the materials we will need in order to change the dressing on Evan's PICC line. We look nervously at the tube and dressing on Evan's upper thigh. We know that this convenient access tube, surgically implanted, has to stay in place for now and the dressing must be changed regularly. It is unnerving to know that an infection in the tube or area of skin around it could go directly to a vein that goes directly to Evan's heart. So we try not to think about this and instead focus on each step of the procedure ahead of us.

We talk through the instructions on the sheet one final time. We discuss who will do what at each stage of the dressing change. We are probably overly cautious about following the directions exactly as they are printed and about keeping everything sterile. That's okay—we are doing everything possible to do our best.

We feel as prepared as we can be. Before we left the hospital, we watched a video, read all the information that was given to us, and received a supervised lesson of an actual complete dressing change on Evan. Now we put our fears and self-doubts aside and begin the process. One by one each step gets completed until we have successfully changed the dressing. Our confidence is boosted and we know that we can continue doing this as long as we need to.

All we can ever ask of ourselves is to try our best. If for some reason you absolutely don't feel capable of doing what is being asked of you, there are some alternative options. You could request an order (through the attending physician at the hospital) for in-home nursing until you feel trained enough to take over. Another possibility would be to speak with your child's pediatrician to find out if you can go into their office for further training or for other suggestions they might have for access to further resources.

Calling the Ambulance

Think about the steps you would take if you were faced with a life-threatening crisis at home. First assess the situation. Is there something you could do immediately such as start CPR or give a breathing treatment? Next be prepared to call 911. It is startling to have to call 911 for the first time. Remember, one of the reasons this service is offered is to help families (such as yours) with special healthcare needs. Make the call and know that your child will get the assistance he needs quickly, emergency first aid will be administered all the way to the hospital, and your child will get admitted directly into the ER—without the delay of the waiting room.

Five weeks old

We have been home from the hospital for eight days, and we are settling into a routine. I have just finished feeding Evan and I am holding him over my shoulder, gently patting his back. I notice he is still and I pull him back to look at his face. His eyes are fixed and he is not breathing. I call to him and pat his back. His face is getting red. He gasps as I work to get him to breathe again. Randy calls 911.

The 911 dispatcher verifies our address and instructs us to turn on the porch light, have someone stand at the door, gather all of his medications, and be ready to go. Evan has been able to gasp for a breath or two but still isn't breathing regularly when the paramedics arrive. They start oxygen, interview us about Evan's medical history, and obtain our insurance information. I call the next-door neighbor who comes over and takes Jonathan to her house.

I hold Evan on my lap in the ambulance. He continues to get oxygen the entire way. Having arrived via ambulance, we are taken immediately into an examination room and intervention begins. After several hours he is breathing easily with oxygen, but he is not ready to go home. He is admitted and moved to the pediatric floor. This is the third hospital we have learned to navigate—first his birth hospital, then the university hospital, and now a local hospital that has a PICU.

Randy visits us at the hospital. He brings extra things we need: the Habermann bottle, formula, food thickeners, clothes for Evan and me, the medical notebook that holds so much vital information, my medications, snacks, and the book I am reading.

As the ER visit stretches into several days, our life is reorganized again. I stay with Evan in the hospital and Randy organizes life at home with Jonathan. For the most part our life is just on hold. My focus again is caring for Evan in the hospital, until he grows strong enough to go home again.

In time you will become confident in understanding how your child responds to illnesses, the conditions that bring about a health crisis, and the interventions that work best. You will know when you are successfully managing a situation at home or when you need to call 911.

Be Prepared

You can do a few things to be prepared for an emergency at home. Three things that we have found helpful include 1) creating a vital information sheet to hand to paramedics, 2) creating an ER backpack with items we'll need, and 3) learning CPR and other techniques we might need to administer (for conditions such as injury, seizure, choking).

Vital information sheet to hand to paramedics could include:

- Child's name, address, date of birth
- Parent's name, address, phone numbers
- Emergency contact name, address, phone numbers
- Medical history information, including:
    - doctor and phone number, preferred hospital, blood type, special conditions and notes, medications (dosage and frequency), list of surgeries, allergies
- Medical insurance information, including company name, policy number, contact information

Backpack with everything you will need

- Feeding necessities: bottles, formula, thickeners
- Extra clothes
- Cash
- Book
- Toys, movies, music for older children
- Small bag of toiletries for parent—toothbrush, toothpaste, etc.

- At the last minute, add parents' and child's medication, phone, wallet

You can obtain training information on CPR and first aid techniques from the hospital your child is in or from your pediatrician. The American Heart Association and The Red Cross both have classes (locally and online) and resources available. Keep books and movies at home and review every couple of months to keep your skills fresh in your mind. You can also find training movies and demonstrations online.

Working with Your Child's Pediatrician

Evan's pediatrician became a steady presence in our lives as our journey at home moved forward. She possessed many qualities that made her an ideal doctor for our situation. She had parenting experience, a calm disposition, an engaging personality, great listening skills, compassion, bright confidence, an openness to new ideas, and extensive medical knowledge. She earned our trust by consistently providing thorough care.

Evan had many appointments at the pediatrician's office the first year: well baby check-ups, follow-up visits after hospital stays, visits to discuss emerging concerns, and treatments for respiratory illnesses.

I was grateful for the caution the office used in caring for Evan. Immediately after we checked in for an office visit, we were brought into an exam room. This limited his exposure to dangerous germs in the waiting room.

We could count on her to closely monitor our trips to the ER. She took time to speak with me on the phone to make sure I felt the staff at the ER understood our complex situation. Whenever possible, she visited us in the ER. She encouraged us to be assertive advocates when working with ER staff and specialists. This proved to be invaluable advice.

She developed a solid understanding of Evan's needs first-hand as she experienced various health events unfolding. During a well baby visit in Evan's first year (a visit when Evan looked and sounded great) she asked what concerns I had that day. I attempted to describe our fear and uncertainty of what to do when Evan's health changed instantly. I explained, "It's so unpredictable—never any gradual symptoms coming on. One minute he is having a good day, the next minute he is sick and having problems breathing. We have to try to figure out what is going on. It can be really challenging to decide what to do. We never know if it is just a passing cough or if it is something heavy settling in. Do we try to care for him at home, or should we take him into the ER?"

She listened, commiserated, and offered some suggestions. We left the subject with an acknowledgment that we had to just take each situation as it came and try to learn how to handle it as time goes on. Evan got his vaccines and we drove home.

Unbelievably, in the fifteen minutes it took to drive home, Evan started wheezing and coughing. Terrified, I thought maybe he was having a reaction to the vaccines. Once I had him inside the house, I realized that he was really struggling to breathe, and thought, *Here we go again.* I called our pediatrician and told her exactly what was happening.

I heard the dismay in her voice as she said, "He was fine just fifteen minutes ago!"

"I know! This is exactly what I was talking about." I put the phone up to Evan's mouth so she could hear it herself. "Do you think it is a reaction to the vaccines?"

"Not likely. This isn't how a reaction presents itself. It sounds like you are going to have to take him into the ER. I'm sorry this is happening. I'm going to try to meet you there—I want to see him myself."

Later, she read his chart in the ER and observed Evan's condition firsthand. Lab work showed he had an acute upper respiratory illness. She shook her head, and we shared a moment of disbelief. "Now I know exactly what you mean. His condition changed instantly. He was fine in the office."

Gradually we pieced together the complicated factors that contributed to these sudden swings, and developed a regime of treatment using steroids. When we moved to a new state in Evan's third year, we were devastated to lose the trusted, steady presence we had in Evan's first pediatrician. But we found other pediatricians who also possess many fine qualities, and who care for Evan in a comprehensive and proactive manner.

Be an Insistent Advocate

Sometimes you will have to be insistent to get what your child needs. If your child's care is not adequate and your concerns aren't being heard, you will have to really focus, get to work, and be persistent. Your child can't speak for himself—it is your job to be your child's voice.

Fourteen weeks old

Up until now, our emergency room experiences have been positive. Evan has received efficient and excellent care. However this ER visit tests our advocacy skills to their maximum limits.

We have brought Evan into the ER for breathing issues. He has a respiratory illness and he is struggling. This particular ER has a separate pediatric unit. But it is closed. Apparently this hospital maximizes resources by only opening the pediatric ER during certain hours.

We are dismayed to have Evan placed in among adults, in a part of the ER where patients are lined up in a row, partitioned off only by drapes. The adult patient on the other side of the drape is vomiting and coughing, with some of it spilling into Evan's area. The situation is completely unacceptable, posing significant danger to Evan's fragile state.

We try everything we can think of to get him moved to an isolated area. We ask the nurses and doctors to move him. We stand outside Evan's area and asked every staff person that passes if Evan could be moved immediately. We ask to speak to the hospital manager. We call our pediatrician. We even take the extreme measure of crossing the line of proper procedure by calling up to the pediatric floor to check if Evan truly is on an admittance list that we were told he is on. He isn't.

Nobody is very happy with us at this point—not the floor staff or the ER staff. However, we finally get results and I will never regret being an aggressive advocate at this point. Evan is moved to an isolated area and soon after that moved to the pediatric floor. Later I learn that an acquaintance, who also has a medically fragile infant, had almost exactly the same experience in this ER and wrote a formal complaint to the hospital.

Unfortunately you might find yourself in bad situations without an easy fix. In these cases you will have to stretch yourself to get whatever it is that your child needs. The experience could take you way out of your comfort zone. However, you must be your child's advocate and voice. You must ensure that your child gets whatever he needs. Dig down deep and fight for whatever that is.

Prioritizing the Reality of Employment

Caring for a medically fragile child is a very expensive proposition. Even with health insurance there are still copays, coinsurance, deductibles, and items that insurance doesn't cover. The expenses of caring for Evan at home began adding up, some of which included:

- Compounded medication (turning a tablet form into a liquid form) which our insurance refused to pay for because it was compounded: $90 monthly

- Prescription copays

- Medical equipment copays

- Doctor visit copays—sometimes multiple visits daily. On average $300–$500 monthly

- Hospital copays—staggering

- Expensive baby formula, the only formula Evan's digestive system could tolerate

- Habermann bottles, which cost $35 each

- Travel expenses to major medical centers

The time had come when we needed to be pragmatic about our employment situation; we needed to be practical, sensible, and make some hard choices. There was no room for missteps in this new life.

Two years earlier we had made the decision that I would take time off from teaching school so that we could raise our children with one parent at home—me. I began teaching music lessons from our home with the thought that someday I would return to teaching school. That was out of the question now for the foreseeable future.

Randy absolutely had to maintain his employment at his two jobs (full-time university choir director and part-time church choir director). He couldn't be up all night and running around all day to doctor's appointments and keep up his work obligations. So we made the decision that we needed me to take over nighttime care and be in charge of all of Evan's treatment needs and we needed Randy to continue to put his energy into his employment.

Taking responsibility for Evan's nighttime care meant I was the primary "stay awake" parent. Randy still helped out during the night and wished that he could shoulder more of this burden. But the reality was that I needed to be on duty the whole night every night, and Randy needed to go to work every day. For me, Evan's first year can be summed up as sleepless. The second year was slightly better.

The two issues that plagued Evan during the night were breathing problems and vomiting. We had a bed next to Evan's crib. I rested in it during the night while listening for the gasping and vomiting that would send me racing into action.

We didn't realize what was happening, but gradually over Evan's first eight months he was developing hydrocephalus. This caused a great deal of discomfort for him and contributed to his nighttime nausea. His head was getting bigger so gradually that nobody realized what was happening. Once a VP shunt was placed at eight months, the nighttime vomiting subsided significantly, but not completely.

I learned to prepare his crib each day in several alternating layers of plastic covers and sheets. As needed throughout the night, I simply peeled away a mess, tossed it in the laundry, and a fresh clean bed was ready and waiting. He would need his middle-of-the-night feeding and the whole process would begin again. I held him and burped him for hours to try to relieve his reflux. I gave breathing treatments to ease the effects of seemingly endless respiratory infections.

When we were in the hospital, I was the one who needed to stay with Evan. The notoriously uncomfortable sleeping chairs and couches seemed blissful me. I fell asleep instantly, knowing that the nurses were monitoring Evan's breathing.

Four months after Evan was born, I began to teach some lessons again. I hired an extremely competent high school student who had become a like a trusted older daughter to babysit while I taught. The time she spent with my kids was the most consistent respite I had. She was confident with Evan and was a breath of fresh air for Jonathan. She played with the kids, cleaned, and cooked. Sometimes she stayed beyond my lessons and I took a nap. While a good portion of my lesson income went to pay for her, it was the break I needed.

Several years later, when Evan was three and we had relocated to a new state, I ventured outside of the house for a part-time administrative job. The part-time job was ideal because some of the work was writing I could do at home. I found two young women, professional caregivers, who alternated coming to our house to care for Evan. Again, a good portion of my income went to pay for these caregivers, but it was the break I needed.

The three years I did this job coincided with a window of time free from major surgeries. I cherished the time away from the pressures of home in which I could stretch my mind and make connections in the community. However, after three years of this employment, I was taking on more work roles and spending more time away from home. I made the choice to leave this position in order to focus on our home life. It was time to prepare for a series of complicated surgeries.

You Don't Get to Be Squeamish

You are your child's pillar of strength. Whatever pain or trauma your child has to deal with, you need to look confident, have a reassuring voice, and hold his hand. He will have to endure all kinds of procedures that most adults couldn't face bravely and you don't get to run away or be squeamish. Whatever clean up or procedure you must perform, be strong, and get it done.

Eight-and-a-half months old

Home from Dallas, Texas, on February 26, 2005, complete with four soft casts after reconstruction surgery on his fingers and toes. Because we live 1,000 miles away from where Evan had surgery, he has been sent home to recover with soft casts—soft casts that we will unwrap and remove ourselves at home after two-and-a-half weeks.

The two-and-a-half weeks of fumbling around with his four cumbersome appendages is about to end. It is time for us to remove the casts and bandages. The job ahead of us is intimidating, never having dealt with the healing process of surgery before. We are nervous about disturbing the incision sites and skin grafts—anxious that we might inflict pain or damage the sores.

But knowing that Evan must move on to the next stage of recovery, we begin to unwrap the layers of bandages until we gingerly peel away the final layer. And there they are—absolutely amazing—tiny, individual fingers and toes, just waiting to go into action. We laugh and cheer in excitement. We capture the moment with pictures.

After this, we apply fresh saline gauze dressings three times a day for ten days. Removing old dressings and weaving new ones in and out around his new digits. And then, miraculously, here they are—little graspers picking up food and toys—full of the promise of independence.

Consider yourself lucky if you already have a tolerance for the more difficult clean ups and procedures. I have found that it is much easier to face these issues immediately and get them done. It is better to discover a problem, face it head on, and take care of it right away, than to avoid a problem and let it fester.

Nighttime and Respiratory Issues

For years we thought that fate was dealing us a bad hand. Night after night, Evan would wake up between 11:00 p.m. and 2:00 a.m., coughing, croupy, and struggling to breathe. We would go into action, questioning the fairness of it all—why couldn't this happen during the day? At least when we were awake, we were prepared to give breathing treatments or run to the ER. We stumbled around half-asleep wondering when this particular type of bad luck would stop visiting us.

Evan was six years old before we finally began to understand this cycle of respiratory distress. We took Evan to be seen by a new specialist and we described Evan's challenging nighttime breathing issues. We shared our sense of mystification at how this always happened to Evan in the middle of the night.

The doctor wasn't mystified at these nighttime spells. He talked about what happens to the human body during the night and why the conditions are just right for what we had been experiencing. While asleep, the body's parasympathetic nervous system works to increase its production of mucus and saliva. The effect of these extra secretions is compounded by the fact that while sleeping, a person is in a lying down position and the soft tissues and muscles are relaxing. The combination of extra secretions, lying down, and relaxed tissues and muscles sets up the perfect conditions for respiratory distress.

At that moment we had a dramatic shift in thinking. Instead of feeling like the victims of bad luck, we felt empowered to be prepared to go into action. We started anticipating when the conditions would be perfect for Evan to get croup during the night. On those nights we added to the bedtime routine, including final breathing treatments, a little antihistamine (according to the doctor's recommendation), and propping him up with more pillows. We set up the nebulizer with albuterol and saline for easy access in the middle of the night. We started going to bed earlier and setting an alarm so we could wake up and check on his breathing. We set out the ER backpack, ready to go just in case.

Now the nighttime episodes are just one more part of our routine; we no longer feel we are victims of an irritating cycle of bad luck. This new understanding has shifted our perception and changed our lives dramatically. Knowledge is power.

Respite Care

Respite care is a very important resource that has helped us sustain our ability to care for our medically fragile child over time. We have found that we all—Evan, too—benefit from having respite care. We are able to take a needed break from the intense pressures of caregiving. Evan is able to take a break from his almost constantly exhausted parents. Additionally, the respite caregivers we have been fortunate enough to work with have taught us many things about caregiving.

Respite care can be received in the home or out of the home in a respite facility. With this respite time you can recharge your energy and have time to sleep, exercise, complete paperwork, organize appointments, care for other children, or run an errand.

Specialized home health companies (some are nonprofit agencies and some are for profit) provide nurses and caregivers for individuals with special healthcare needs. These services may be covered by Medicaid (for eligible individuals) or can be paid for out of pocket. Additionally, certain organizations may provide short-term grants to fund respite care during an emergency. The United Way provided us with a month of respite care (two hours daily) at a time when I had a back injury and couldn't lift Evan or perform the caregiving that needed to be done. If you have 211 service in your location, they may have information about organizations that could help. Other affordable ways for you to receive respite care include asking friends, family, and your church.

To find more information on all aspects of respite care, you can visit the ARCH National Respite Network and Resource Center at www.Archrespite.org.

Here are a few ideas to begin your search locally for respite care.

- www.Archrespite.org—find the search tool for locating providers by state.

- Search your county website; look under Child and Family Services.

- Look in the yellow pages under Home Health Services.

- Contact individual organizations active in your community whose mission is to serve children with special healthcare needs (such as a CP Center, United Way, March of Dimes, or Easter Seals).

Individuals with Disabilities Education Act

Many children with special healthcare needs qualify for educational services and early intervention services under the Individuals with Disabilities Education Act (IDEA). To fully understand how your child might benefit from this federal law, I strongly recommend that you visit the website for the National Dissemination Center for Children with Disabilities, www.nichcy. org. Here you will find a vast amount of information, including: descriptions of categories of disabilities, developmental milestones, explanation of the special education process (for babies and toddlers, and for ages 3–22), laws, research papers, state organizations, etc. The National Dissemination Center for Children with Disabilities is funded by the Office of Special Education Programs through the US Department of Education.

Each state is responsible for providing services, according to the federal law IDEA. Part C (Early Intervention) ensures that services are available for children, from birth until they turn three. Through Early Intervention, your child may have access to a range of therapists and teachers, depending on his or her specific disability. If your child is eligible to receive services, an IFSP (Individualized Family Service Plan) will be written for your child. This plan will outline what services your child will receive (for example, speech therapy, occupational therapy, physical therapy, audiology services, assistive technology devices, and other assistance).

Evan qualified for various services as an infant. Receiving these services has played a vital role in his development. I made these therapies a priority and took part in the weekly therapy sessions in order to learn how to continue practicing throughout the week. Additionally, I took photos and made a binder outlining what was being worked on so that other family members and respite caregivers could also continue to practice the work.

Keep a History Record

Each new specialist you see will want you to brief them on your child's most significant health information. Be prepared to provide this information by keeping an ongoing health history summary. I keep a copy in my notebook and update periodically.

First I list all the doctors Evan sees. I include addresses, phone numbers, and fax numbers. This information is used to share appointment notes and to facilitate the process of doctors contacting each other to consult as necessary. I am always thankful to have this information when I am filling out the paperwork required by all doctors.

Next I list all of Evan's significant health events chronologically: hospitalizations, major illnesses, surgeries, treatments that were tried (what worked and what didn't), and current medications.

This summary helps me to organize my thoughts and to know that I am sharing information accurately. It also helps me see patterns in Evan's growth, and cycles of illnesses and sensitivities.

Online Support Groups

We have found online support groups to be extremely helpful. We are thankful to have the ability to connect with other parents who are dealing with similar issues. The online support groups provide a convenient way to ask questions, find support, and understand issues we encounter. I especially appreciate the hope I find in the notes written by adults with Apert syndrome. It is exciting to think of Evan growing up and contributing to society as an independent adult.

eight

CARING FOR SIBLINGS

Evan, Are You Better?

Evan, are you better?
Better I say better?
Maybe with this letter
You will feel much better.

~Poem by Jonathan age 7, written for Evan age 5

A New Normal

Children are resilient and can adapt to just about anything life hands them. A wide body of research has shown that children who struggle with difficult situations can actually benefit from those struggles as adults. They tend to develop life skills that help them function successfully in the real world. They usually become independent thinkers with the ability to adapt to life's challenges.

Evan is four years old and Jonathan is six years old

We worry that Jonathan is being neglected or somehow robbed of the idyllic childhood that we had. We take him to meet with a psychologist, part of our efforts to make sure that he is getting everything he needs. The first time we meet with this doctor, we tell her we are concerned that Jonathan is suffering in some way from being on the sidelines while we struggle with Evan. We are afraid that the stress is affecting his personality and causing him to be overly impulsive and sensitive. She responds, "No. Jonathan's life as Evan's brother is normal to him. You can't worry about that. Everyone has something stressful in life, and we all adapt. Jonathan is Jonathan because that is who he is. He was born with certain talents and personality traits. He isn't developing these traits because of Evan. Think of how he was as a baby. Can you remember some of these strong tendencies being present in him, even as a baby?" And she is right. It is true that Jonathan's personality has been consistent since birth.

It is also true that because of our family situation, Jonathan has had a unique opportunity to experience the world with a deep appreciation for life and to develop a broad understanding of the human condition.

For Jonathan, this has meant developing a gentle nature, compassion, and empathy. He is flexible and knows that plans can change in a heartbeat. He is a thoughtful teacher. He is a protector. He is his own person and our life with Evan is his normal.

Keep Children on a Routine

Children love routine. They thrive within a routine, secure in the knowledge that every day has a predictable pattern.

Here is the routine that I developed for Jonathan, age two. Evan was a newborn being cared for in the hospital and our lives were in complete upheaval. Jonathan took it all in stride, each day unfolding in a similar way as the last.

7:00 a.m   Wake up, change diaper, put on clothes, make bed, eat breakfast

8:00 a.m.   Play-time with Mom

10:00 a.m. Snack time

10:30 a.m   Babysitter: play outside, or outing, or playroom

12:00 p.m. Lunch

12:30 p.m. Nap

2:30 p.m.   (Or whenever he gets up) Spend time alone in room, reading books or playing with toys

3:30 p.m.   Babysitter: Play outside, or outing, or playroom

5:00 p.m.   Video

5:30 p.m.   Dinner with Dad

6:30 p.m.   Family time (quiet playtime with adults)

7:30-8:00 Bedtime (Bath, pajamas on, brush teeth, read book in Mommy and Daddy's room, say "Off to bed" and go to Jonathan's bed, say prayers)

You are Important

Nothing says, "You are important to me," more than giving someone your undivided attention and time. Think about your own experiences with family and friends. How does it feel when your favorite people spend time with you? Are there people you want to spend more time with, but they never have time for you? What message does this send to you?

The same is true with our children (the people we love most in the world). You send the message "You are important to me" to your children when you spend quality time with them.

We call it Jonathan and Mommy Time, or Jonathan and Daddy Time, or Family Time. We do simple things, nothing extravagant, and we give our undivided attention and time. We do the same thing with Evan. We just make extra sure that Jonathan gets his fair share.

Simple ways to share time with your children

- Play board games or card games.
- Read a book—a longer novel that will take many sessions of enjoying the story together is fun (along with the promise of "to be continued").
- Paint watercolor pictures.
- Play a lawn game, basketball, or tennis.
- Take a picnic.
- Go on a walk.
- Learn origami.
- Watch a movie.
- Go fishing or camping.

You are Special, Too

Children need to know that they are special and that they have an important place in the world. To parents, it is obvious that our children are special. We are so proud of each accomplishment. We praise our children often, maybe too much. But no matter how much praise and encouragement we give, it is never enough to completely erase insecurities, self-doubts, and questions of self-worth.

Evan is two years old and Jonathan is four years old

Introducing Evan to new people is awkward. What do you say to someone staring at his unusual appearance, without ignoring that awkward moment or initiating a big discussion? I have fallen into the habit of introducing the boys by saying, "This is Jonathan, and he is four. And this is Evan, my special little guy, he is two." This is my way of acknowledging that Evan has special needs and special looks. It seems to put the new acquaintance at ease, without telling too much.

As we walk away from just such a meeting, I realize too late that Jonathan has begun mastering the art of conversation and word nuances. He pipes in with, "Mommy, I'm special, too. Aren't I?" I stop in my tracks and look at him looking up at me. I wasn't expecting that. How long had he been mulling that one over? At four he is already contemplating his place in the family.

I took it for granted that he knew that Evan was born different and that special was one way to describe that. I try to explain this to Jonathan—but to him Evan is normal, not special. In Jonathan's world, Evan being singled out as special has the direct implication that he might not be special.

So I stop using the easy, comfortable introduction that I had begun to rely on, and I leave out the qualifiers.

I gradually realize that they weren't necessary; adults don't need to be made comfortable. They can take care of themselves.

Each child is exceptional. Each child needs to know that his parents believe he is a treasure and that he holds a unique place in this world. Make sure that in the whirlwind of caring for your special needs child, all of your children know that they are special, too.

Hugs and Kisses, I Love You

No matter what each day holds, always have a hug, a kiss, and an "I love you" for your children. Love is the magic ingredient that holds a family together through pain and turmoil. As much as you try to protect your children from the stress of your life, you also have to reassure them with positive acts of love.

We have a ritual that begins each morning. When the kids wake up and find us, we smile warmly, give a hug, and say, "Good morning." We start the morning choosing to be happy and intending to have a good day.

Evan is five years old and Jonathan is seven years old

For a long time I avoided looking anyone in the eye. Not deliberately, but rather subconsciously, protecting others and myself from my pain. Instinctively I knew that if my pain were revealed, if someone saw something telling in my eyes, there would be the possibility that my emotions would be given the opportunity to run out of their containment unchecked. The possibility of crumbling into little pieces at any moment was real, and I needed to keep that from happening.

Jonathan is the person that I have worked hardest to hide my pain from, to protect him from the hard reality of our life. For years I would only let my eyes quickly meet his, then move on, preventing him from seeing—from even just sensing—his mommy's pain. He was six or seven years old before I was able to try to hold his gaze. At that time I was stronger, my pain was more distant, and I was happier.

When I did begin to seek out his eye contact, I realized that Jonathan wasn't comfortable looking me in the eye. His eyes avoided my eyes, and most other people's eyes, too.

Maybe Jonathan is just wired to avoid making direct eye contact. Maybe he has learned this from me. Maybe he is protecting himself from acknowledging the pain he senses in all of our hearts. Most likely it is a combination of all of these ideas.

These days I practice holding his gaze, attempting to reassure him with my eyes that we are all in a good place and that we are at peace with our life just as it is. The moments are now savored and they grow easier, filled with more confidence and more contentment.

How much pain should we protect our children from? First and foremost, we need to assure our children that everything is okay and that each day is a chance for new joy. I suspect that no matter how hard we try to protect our children, they are such sensitive creatures that they know when we are in pain.

Children Learn What They See

Whenever we take Evan out we are confronted with children who are befuddled by his appearance. We see quizzical looks in his direction and hear, "Look at that boy. His head looks funny. Why is his head so big?" The script is almost the same every time. The parents try to quiet them, making the mystery all that more intriguing.

I pull Evan close to me, smile, and kiss him, understanding that the parents have no idea how to handle the situation. Then I get down to the kid's level and say, "This is Evan. Would you like to meet him? He is my little boy. He was born with Apert syndrome. That means he was born looking a little different on the outside than most people. But on the inside he is exactly the same as everybody else. He has feelings, he laughs, and he cries. What is your name? Annie, this is Evan. Evan, this is Annie." Evan smiles, wins their hearts and says, "Hi Annie." And we go back to playing until someone else passes us and we start all over again.

Time and time again, Jonathan has stood next to us while we share Evan and educate the public about who he is. We have never turned away from difficult situations with people who are curious or agitated by Evan's appearance. We seize the moment to connect, educate, and advocate.

Evan is seven years old and Jonathan is nine years old
Jonathan waits in line to get on a ride at an amusement park. Randy and Evan stand off to the side, Evan is not big enough for this ride. Jonathan is excited to be going on the ride with the special audience of his dad and little brother watching. His attention is drawn to the two boys standing in line in front of him (who are obviously older than he is) and his world suddenly comes to a stop as he realizes they are making fun of Evan. Evan is just far enough away that the boys feel comfortable joking about his unusual looks.

Jonathan doesn't turn away. He doesn't pretend that he can't hear or see what is going on. He doesn't disown his brother. He stands up tall, gets the boys' attention, and says to them, "I would be happy to know that you aren't talking about that little boy over there. Because, if you are, that is my little brother." The boys are stunned and obviously embarrassed. Each accuses the other of doing the unkind acts and then claim that they are just talking about the movie Frankenstein. Jonathan knows better, and they know it, too. Thankfully, it is time to get on the ride and they all escape the difficult situation.

Later, I ask Jonathan why he didn't tell them about Evan and Apert syndrome. He says, "Mom, I was just so angry. That was all I could do. I was just filled with anger so much that I couldn't say anything else."

In the only way his emotions allowed at the time, Jonathan connected, educated, and advocated. He imitated the way we have handled similar situations. Never forget that your children are watching, listening, and learning as you navigate through these difficult situations. Have a kind and understanding heart (try to rein in hurt and anger) as you teach the world about human differences.

Don't Worry Too Much

My friend Holly visited me and said, "My mother has a message for you. She says to tell you not to worry too much. She wants you to know that the thing she regrets most about raising my brother is that she worried too much. Do all that you can do, and know that it is enough."

Holly's mother was carrying a healthy, normally developing child until she was unknowingly exposed to German measles by a relative. As a result of contracting this illness in utero, Holly's brother was born profoundly deaf, and with a life-threatening heart defect as well as other serious health complications. It was a tragedy that struck her family deeply at a time when little support was available for children with special needs.

Through this ordeal, Holly's parents had significant financial, healthcare, and emotional challenges to deal with. Holly's mother worried about her children having everything they needed (shoes, clothes, food, healthcare). She worried about her son's health and all of his special needs. She worried about having enough energy to care for him when she and her husband worked long hours in physically demanding jobs. Holly often sat by her brother's side so that her mother could sleep for a few hours. Most of all, Holly's mother worried about her ability to do everything humanly possible to give her son everything he needed to learn and develop into an independent adult.

"I am inexpressibly proud of my brother," Holly says as she tells his story. "He overcame many physical and social obstacles to become a kind, dependable person who exhibits grace under pressure and sees the humor in any situation. With the use of two powerful hearing aids he successfully navigates the hearing world and communicates well, speaking only with what people perceive as a slight accent. He holds two college degrees from the University of Maryland, a number of technical certifications, and is in the midst of a long and successful career in information technology.

"Some time ago, my brother and I were remembering childhood events with our mother. She began to express regret for all of the ways in which she felt she had let us both down as she and my father strove to cope with the social, emotional, and financial challenges of raising a child with exceptional needs. My brother and I looked at each other and he said, 'Mom, I wish you hadn't worried about it so much. Holly and I never did. Children are resilient. You and Dad loved us and did your best for us and we had lots of good times along with the tough ones. We've always been okay.'"

No one can predict the future. All you have is today. And today you will have smiles, hugs, kisses, and moments of joy only a child can share.

nine

CARING FOR YOUR MARRIAGE

Stronger

Seven years old

We are different now—stronger in many ways. Perhaps our innocent optimism is gone, but other more mature traits have taken its place. We are more forgiving and understanding (being right doesn't really matter anymore; that's a good thing). We are more tolerant and patient. We are more creative.

Each of us has had to grow in our relationship. We have learned that under stress our personalities are magnified. However we cope or tend to be, it is more. We have had to take ownership of our own personalities and work to be more flexible. We have had to move into a whole new level of acceptance of each other's personalities. From there, we have had to figure out how to make our personalities work together and complement each other. This is where our success lies. We are good at different things, in different ways, and at different times. Between the two of us, everything manages to get done.

There is no one else in the world who knows just how strong each of us has had to become in order to survive since Evan was born. We find ways to bolster that strength (always building up, never tearing down). Mostly we are content, feeling fortunate for another day of good health. We are thankful for a day that is uneventful, basking in the serenity of stability.

Therapy

We didn't fully understand it at the time, but the moment we became parents of a medically fragile child we entered into a family crisis. Our lives were in complete upheaval. Over time we learned new skills to survive this dramatic shift in our lives. We put aside any stigma of mental health care that we had, and we investigated the possibility of finding a counselor who could teach us how to manage our crisis. We learned that counseling shouldn't be viewed as a last resort effort—something drastic to be implemented when all else fails. Counseling should be considered in the beginning of a crisis—early enough in the experience to learn the life skills necessary to survive all of the trials ahead of you.

One year old

We have settled into an irritated edginess. The never-ending pressure, sleepless nights, worry, grief, and self-doubt are the biggest players—all working together to bring us down. We try to give each other a lot of leeway. We know that at any moment our lives could just unravel. We both agree that we need to learn new skills to keep our marriage and our family together.

We have found a counselor that we both like. She sees each of us individually, then together. We take personality tests, so that we can understand how each of us thinks and reacts to the world around us. Suddenly, our recent interactions with each other make sense. We realize that our underlying personalities have been magnified under all the stress. What used to be little quirks are now serious roadblocks in our ability to communicate and function at our best. We learn to be aware of our typical coping mechanisms, to analyze whether or not these modes of operation are effective, and to think objectively about how this impacts our partner. We learn how to nurture our relationship while under this intense stress. We remember to be kinder and more understanding of each other.

We learn to acknowledge our own failures and begin to laugh at ourselves, knowing that our own personality can get us into trouble once in a while. We survive in the face of great trials with an even stronger bond than ever.

In counseling, you will have the opportunity to grow individually and as a family. You will explore new ways to communicate and interact with each other in order to have increased empathy and understanding. You will have a mediator to diffuse anger in the most difficult times. You will find positive ways to survive what could be the most pivotal point in your relationship.

Be Nice

When it feels like the world is beating us up, we welcome each other's compassion and ability to just be nice. It is so simple, but just being nice to each other has the power to alleviate anxiety, calm nerves, and make everything okay for a moment. The quality of our lives will be determined largely by the quality of time we spend together as a couple. Although it is easy to mindlessly take our frustrations and anger out on each other, we mindfully try not to. We try to do whatever it takes to put the pressures of our lives aside and be a comfort for each other.

Types of strategies we use to be comforting to each other

We surprise each other by doing small thoughtful things for each other: bring a cup of coffee, arrive home with a treat, offer to do an errand that the other doesn't have time to do.

- We are appreciative of unexpected thoughtful gestures.
- We are willing to do whatever it takes to resolve misunderstandings and mistakes.
- We are patient listeners and we try to be open to different perspectives.
- We attempt to share our feelings without accusing each other of wrongdoings.
- We accept each other's feelings as something meaningful.
- We give free passes to each other.
- We are forgiving and we let go of hurt feelings.

Equal and fair are words that probably need to be thrown out the door. We realized very early on that if we kept track of who did what, it would consume both of us. In order to survive, each of us is good at different things and at different times. We accept this, we appreciate what the other does, and we acknowledge each other's contributions.

Understand that you both will make mistakes—no one will be free of fault all of the time. Give each other opportunities to repair mistakes. As a couple, you will rely on each other to be there in the tough times. Go above and beyond to treat your partner kindly. You are each other's strongest supporter.

Time Together

Our life as a couple must go on, despite all the realities of being a parent of a medically fragile child. Sharing a carefree moment or outing with someone you love is what life is all about. It may seem like carefree moments and outings are luxuries that should be put on hold for now and reserved for easier times. But really, when is it going to get easier? Your whole life could pass you by, while you wait for easier times. Today is all that any of us have; there is no guarantee what tomorrow will bring for anyone.

Set aside a time each week to focus on having fun together as a couple. Don't discuss illnesses, medical bills, appointments, or anything stressful. Share a silly book or funny movie. Do something active or just collapse in a quiet restaurant.

Be creative. If all you can afford is a babysitter, then pack a picnic and go to a park. Take a walk. Find a restaurant that fits your budget. Or leave the kids at the babysitter's house, and you stay home and have pizza and a movie.

If you can't find or afford a babysitter, put the kids to bed early and enjoy some takeout, candlelight, and nice music. We have found that the earlier we put the kids to bed, the easier it is. As the night gets later it gets progressively harder because tired kids are cranky kids. So make it easier on everyone and put the kids to bed early.

Cherish this weekly time together; it is vital to your survival as a couple.

Time Spent Separately

The energy of being with someone who is not a family member intricately bound by this medical crisis is rejuvenating. Spending time with a good friend is important. Make time to get out of the house with a friend, change your focus for a time, laugh, and be free of the stress.

There are some things you can share with a friend that you can't share with your partner: things that women talk about together and things that men talk about together, common interests, common challenges.

There are activities we enjoy that are important parts of who we are, but that we don't share the same interest in. Randy might want company fishing or watching a sporting event. I might rather spend the time doing a craft project. We are happy for each other when we get an opportunity to do these things, even though we don't enjoy them together.

For similar reasons time spent alone is equally important. Everybody needs a certain amount of solitude. Time spent alone can be used to care for yourselves and to further pursue your individual interests. Your life must go on, despite the crisis all around you.

I have included *Time Spent Separately* in *Strategies to Care for Your Marriage* for a crucial reason. Randy and I have both experienced times with our own friends or in solitude that have been rejuvenating and given us the energy to face another day. Because of this, we value these experiences for ourselves and for each other. We make it possible for each of us to have these times, while being respectful of the time afforded to us away from the pressures of home and family.

Measuring Success

Before Evan, the goals we had for our marriage and the future seemed to be focused on what we hoped to accumulate. As newlyweds, our thoughts were focused on getting to a certain place in our life where we would be living in the perfect house, have the perfect stuff, take the perfect vacations, and then enjoy all that we had achieved by planning rather sophisticated social events with our friends. If magazines or home TV shows are any indication, we aren't the only young couple that has had these ideas. In our commercialized society, we are programmed to think this way.

As teachers, there never would have been a perfect time for this medically induced financial crisis to hit us. This crisis (compounded by youth, graduate school, and two cross-country moves) has stripped us of every spare cent we had.

One thing my children absolutely need to know is that I don't care about the money (or lack of it). The joy these two boys have brought us far outweighs every penny we have spent to make their lives successful. Moreover, I am glad that the boys are being raised with values that don't revolve around money and buying things.

For example, one Christmas, Evan desperately wanted a dollhouse. Jonathan and I decided to make one for him. We spent the month of December creating an elaborate dollhouse out of shoeboxes and recycled materials, complete with boy-colored wallpaper and handmade accessories. It was an incredibly creative time for us as we thought through each stage of the project. On top of that, Jonathan and I bonded as we created this surprise that we knew Evan would be ecstatic over.

Creativity is a skill money just can't buy. One winter Randy built two little tables for me out of scrap wood—without a pattern or special accessories. I love those two tables more than our most expensive pieces of furniture. There is such a sense of satisfaction in creating something out of what we have on hand.

I remember a story told to me by a friend who went on a mission to South America. This friend stayed in the home of a villager of very simple means. The villager was getting dressed to go to work and the friend noticed that the villager only owned one shirt. The villager told the friend, "Every day I thank God that I have a shirt to wear. One shirt is all I need." This story always reminds me that I have more than enough. I am thankful for what I have and I remember not to yearn for things I don't have.

Our small house and our limited belongings have been a blessing during our busiest times. We can easily maintain our things and devote most of our time and energy to our kids, our marriage, and ourselves.

As a couple, Randy and I have had to come to terms with a new focus for our marriage. It is not about how much stuff we can accumulate or what new things we can provide for the boys. It is about living in the moment and enjoying each day for the experiences we have.

ten

FINAL THOUGHTS

We Have Come a Long Way

Evan is seven years old now and the calm periods are longer between his various critical health issues. Evan is stronger and better able to fight off viruses, infections, and ongoing respiratory issues. We are entering a new phase of his development that is focused on his success in school as a first grader.

Kindergarten was all about making good friends (and he made many!). He struggled to stay healthy and missed two-thirds of the school year because of illness and surgery. He was so sad to miss his last two days of the year, including kindergarten graduation, because of a respiratory virus. His teacher saved the day by gathering his class and their fifth grade buddies and marching the entire group from school to our front yard. Evan sat grinning in our picture window as the kids waved, cheered their greetings, and held signs with the words, "We love you Evan." The moment was so poignant that it brought tears to all the adults' eyes.

Evan's treatment for Apert syndrome continues. At age six he underwent a posterior cranial vault, a surgery that reconstructed the back half of his skull. Soon we will find out when he will have his next surgery, the mid-face advancement. A halo device will be surgically implanted around his head and, over a period of three months, his mid-face bones will gradually be moved forward, creating a safer facial structure for his airways. It will also most likely erase most of the signature Apert facial characteristics. In the long run this will be best for him socially. But I will miss his adorable face as it is now.

Other surgeries that Evan has endured include two syndactyly releases (separating his fused fingers and toes), an anterior cranial vault, placement of a VP (ventriculoperitoneal) shunt for hydrocephalus, a cleft palate repair, and five sets of ear tubes. Evan now wears hearing aids and glasses.

Words could never describe the absolute zeal that Evan has for life. It is boundless and contagious. Meeting Evan is life-altering. Seeing the joy that radiates from him while watching him work harder to do everything that most people take for granted (walking with shaky balance, using his fingers which have no joints, discerning sounds through a moderate hearing loss, speaking with an impediment) creates a renewed energy for each of us to be a better person. It reminds those of us who do not have special healthcare needs how lucky we are. It also reminds us that life is to be lived, enjoyed, and cherished.

Everybody Has Challenges

Nobody is without personal challenges, however perfect he or she may seem. Each of us will experience the world with some struggles, which we learn to deal with in our own way, adapting to overcome the challenges we face.

A friend held Evan when he was an infant. She gazed at him and said, "What a miracle Evan is. What a miracle that any of us are here." I thought she was just making conversation, probably at a loss for what to say. "When you really stop to think of how humans are created from tiny cells, it is an absolute miracle. I had three miscarriages and was never able to have a baby of my own. The process is so complicated—it's mind boggling, isn't it? Evan is a miracle." She was talking from her heart.

We are realizing that most people have faced some sort of challenge in their lives. When we can't see someone else's personal trials they tend to go unnoticed. Mistakenly, we believe that life is somehow easier for other people. Because our challenges are so visible, we find that people are compelled to share their own stories with us. They do this partly as catharsis and partly to assure us that we don't struggle alone. Many people have confided in us that seeing Evan triumph so joyfully over his struggles has inspired them to rise above their own.

Realizing that at some point in time everybody will face some sort of challenge has been one of the most important defenses for us in overcoming any bitterness we may have had about the difficulties we face. Understanding that it is our turn to step into the harsh reality that life presents is a big part of accepting our new life and letting go of the old.

Accept and appreciate the miracle of life, complete with imperfections. Allow yourself to connect with other people who know through experience that with challenges comes a richer life and a deeper understanding of the human condition.

Let New People into Your Life

My friends and family are my greatest treasures. Since Evan has come into our lives, we have been given the gift of experiencing relationships in a more meaningful way than ever before. With the barriers of normalcy broken down around us, there has been room for friends and family to step into our lives in a truly magical way.

It is a great comfort to have our friends and family near us and supporting us in so many ways. However, we try to remain mindful to not always focus our conversation on the challenges and to spend plenty of time celebrating the wonder that each day brings.

I explained to a counselor that I fear over-burdening our friends and family with our struggles. She answered back, "Why? Everyone wants a friend who has experienced pain and difficulties. Nobody wants a friend who hasn't experienced the things in life that make us stronger, more compassionate, more knowing. We want friends who have known real pain in life, because those are the friends who really understand our own pain. That's what friends are for—to be there for each other when the going gets rough."

Four years old. Easter Sunday, 2007

It is nearly one year since we relocated to a new town. I am sitting on the stage of the Performing Arts Center with fellow singers in the church choir I recently joined. Even though I don't know many people well, I am thankful to be part of a glorious musical celebration on this beautiful spring morning.

After a set of rousing hymns, the pastor begins his sermon. He tells a story about a man who had captured a small town's heart. This man loved to ride his bike through his town waving and smiling to his neighbors and the people downtown. He had a happy-go-lucky personality that cheered everyone along the way.

The pastor often stopped to talk with the man. One day he invited the man to come to church. The man's face fell as he said, "I will never go to church again. I have asked God over and over for something, but he never answers my prayers."

The pastor asked if the man would share with him what it was that he asked for. The man replied, "I asked God to take away everything from my face that shows that I have Down's syndrome."

I stop hearing the sermon and I feel as though my heart is breaking. My mind freezes with the thought: Will there come a day when Evan agonizes over his appearance? Will there come a day when Evan longs to be more normal and decides he is mad at God for the way he looks? Uncontrollable tears roll down my cheeks. I grab the hand of the soprano sitting next to me, acutely aware of the 1,000 people in the audience, and with nowhere to hide. Although she doesn't know me well, she squeezes my hand back and brings her other hand down on top of both our hands. She gives me the strength to get through the rest of the sermon. We stand and sing the final hymns.

This moment bound our hearts together in a way I imagine few people ever get to experience. In the time since this day we have discovered that we are kindred spirits in many ways. This friendship is a gift, a treasure that can be mostly attributed to all the struggles I had with Evan, leading up to that moment in time.

I didn't hear the rest of the sermon. I was too immersed in my thoughts and trying to act like I wasn't upset in front of 1,000 people. I suspect the lesson in the sermon is that we won't always have control over whether or not certain things happen to us in life. But we can choose to allow unexpected experiences to bring new treasures of friendship.

Continue to Grow

I have become intensely aware of how precious my own accomplishments and goals in life are. Not just for me, but also for my children. I have been given a life that has led me to spend a great deal of time reflecting on the meaning of life's experiences and the value that each person brings to this world. I ponder the value of my own life and understand that while I am first and foremost a parent and caregiver, I am also the producer of my own creative experience.

My heart and mind still want to grow and experience new challenges related to all the things that are me: teaching, singing, playing the piano, writing, gardening, being a part of a community. My desire to learn and to be creative inspires me to get up each day and live a joyful and productive life.

Sometimes I feel as though I am being selfish when I take time to grow my professional and recreational skills. The nagging feeling that I should be focusing all my attention on my family is always there. But then I remember that my main goal with my children is to inspire them to become independent adults who live happy and meaningful lives. Because children learn by example, I choose to continue to grow in all the ways that make me who I am and to live an inspired life. I try to model what a productive adult is, so that my children can learn through my example and find great pleasure in working, creating, and making a joyful home.

I remind myself that it isn't good for children to always be the center of their parents' attention. When children are allowed to play by themselves or with siblings and friends, they grow more independent. When children see that their parents have needs too, they learn empathy and patience.

Certainly I must generate income to support my child with special needs, most likely for his entire life. I must also plan for the possibility that my child may outlive me and he will still need to be taken care of.

I know that the experiences I have had with Evan have made me stronger and smarter; these experiences have empowered me in many ways. I am choosing to use these newly acquired skills to make my life exactly what I want it to be. I am hopeful that someday my children will feel compelled to succeed in wonderful and amazing ways. So, too, can your new life be a new beginning and have the potential for a time of great personal growth.

Embrace a New Life Perspective

Embrace a new life perspective. Evan has awakened in our family a deep appreciation for the joy of each moment. We are learning how to cherish the present moment, and let go of excessive planning for tomorrow or the worry about yesterday.

More than anything else, Evan thrives in living in the present moment. Everything is here and now. Evan's kindergarten teacher told us she loved the way he took each new worksheet assignment and exclaimed with excitement, "I get to do this?!" Worksheets of any kind are an honor. At home, setting the table is a treasured ritual. Even better, decorating the house for a birthday or special holiday is cause for celebration in itself. Meeting new people and going places is the height of a great day. Everything new is fun and exciting and full of joy.

In many ways, it is acknowledging the joy in these otherwise mundane tasks that has made life more real to us. Our family has experienced a relief in letting go of the larger-than-life expectations that society had somehow placed on us, before we had a special needs child. We let go of the wild and crazy movement to do every activity or experience that was available to our family, and we haven't looked back.

I believe we are all happier for doing only what is manageable, what makes us content as a family, and for letting go of activities we felt obligated by society to participate in. We feel fulfilled as a family with no angst about *what else is there?* Or *what is the meaning of our lives?* Or *will we ever get a chance to stop running around and slow down?*

I like to imagine the life that my grandparents lived, and take comfort in the things they enjoyed in simpler times: family gatherings, games, reading, a home cooked meal, music, visiting friends. Modern life takes us farther and farther away from these satisfying ways to enjoy life that sustained families for generations.

Contentment can be found in the most trying of situations. What it all depends on is your mindset—your willingness to embrace what you have and your ability to enjoy each moment as a valuable part of your experience in this life.

ACKNOWLEDGMENTS

My deepest thanks to the following people for their generous contributions to this book: Evan, for changing my life forever in wonderful ways and being my Ambassador of Joy; Randy, for providing limitless encouragement and time to write; Jonathan, for sharing your experiences as a big brother, your enthusiasm, your patience, and your poetry; Terry Stanley, for painting Evan's portrait and capturing his joyful personality—also, for sharing your creative genius in the Uncommon Beauty Project; Kathy Nelson, for sharing your knowledge about the health insurance industry and providing a caring hand to hold; Holly Keaton, for sharing your writings about being the sister of a child with extraordinary medical needs; Victoria Barkell, for encouraging me to dig deeper and share more of my heart; Julia Potter, Liz Schrock, and Peter Jackson for assisting me with rough drafts; Margaret Jackson for your enthusiasm and support; Peggy Morse for your love and support; James Monroe, graphic designer, for your artistic intuition and making everything beautiful; Marly Cornell, my editor, for your deep understanding of the subject matter, your warm yet candid mentoring style, and your magnificent editorial skills; Lily Coyle, my project manager, for your belief in my project, knowing exactly what to say, and overseeing many important details; and all the individuals at Beaver's Pond Press who helped turn my idea into a finished product.

ABOUT THE AUTHOR

Margaret Meder grew up in Madison, Wisconsin. She attended the University of Wisconsin-Madison, earning a bachelor of music degree in 1990. She spent the next sixteen years teaching general and vocal music in the public schools and private lessons. During this time she worked with young children, teenagers, and individuals with special needs. Expanding on these experiences as an educator and musician, Margaret served three years as development director for a nonprofit fine arts organization.

Discovering a void in practical resources on how to survive as a parent of a medically fragile child, Margaret combined her education skills, her love of writing, and her own experiences to create this resource. Her mission is to create accessible resources that provide information, understanding, and inspiration for all parents who find themselves in similar situations. While raising her two children, Margaret pursues the joys in her life: writing, gardening, singing, playing the piano, and—most of all—spending time with her family and friends.

She continues the journey that was started with this book on her blog:

UncommonBeautyCrisisParenting.com

Uncommon Beauty

The day that my friend Terry Stanley, portrait artist, first met Evan was the day she knew that her heart was forever changed. She was immediately inspired to capture his joyful spirit on canvas with a project called *Uncommon Beauty*. Terry painted his portrait in a way that illustrates the profound essence of a child triumphing over significant health challenges. The painting was unveiled at a community Gallery Night, with Evan standing proudly next to his portrait.

The goals of the *Uncommon Beauty* project include increasing understanding of the beauty within disabled children, creating advocacy for the disabled, educating the public about conditions that disabled children live with, and inspiring a new appreciation for inner gifts in all of us—even in the face of complicated challenges.

We hope that Evan's portrait, and perhaps a series of portraits featuring other children, will one day be displayed in universities and hospitals to reach a broad audience and meet these goals.